D1033586

JACKIE ROBINSON

THE 1975 WORLD SERIES

BASEBALL'S
GAME CHANGERS

NIGHT BASEBALL THE YEAR

BABE
RUTH

OF THE PITCHER

HANK AARON

DESIGNATED HITTER

INSTANT REPLAY

BASEBALL'S
GAME CHANGERS
Icons, Record Breakers, Scandals, Sensational Series, and More

GEORGE CASTLE

GUILFORD, CONNECTICUT

An imprint of Rowman & Littlefield

Distributed by NATIONAL BOOK NETWORK

British Library Cataloguing in Publication Information Available

Library of Congress Cataloging-in-Publication Data is available on file.

ISBN 978-1-4930-1946-5 (paperback)
ISBN 978-1-4930-1947-2 (e-book)   **33614059716844**

♾™ The paper used in this publication meets the minimum requirements of American National Standard for Information Sciences—Permanence of Paper for Printed Library Materials, ANSI/NISO Z39.48-1992.

CONTENTS

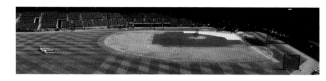

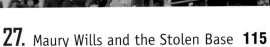

INTRODUCTION
In a Game of Legends, We Love Rankings

The best team ever? The 1927 Yankees or 1975–76 Big Red Machine? Who's the better player? Willie, Mickey, or The Duke? How do we rank the all-time lefties? Some combination of Koufax, Spahn, and the Big Unit? Who's the best broadcaster: Scully, Allen, Costas, Brennaman, or Caray? What is the best baseball movie: *Field of Dreams*, *Bull Durham*, *Pride of the Yankees*, or *Major League*?

Lists and rankings. I could go on and on. With a rich history and romanticism that scarcely exist elsewhere in sports, baseball has had its aficionados pitting one personality or institution of the game against another since the cracker barrel yielded to the water cooler and the Internet.

Many times the arguments are never settled. And in that situation, it's always in keeping with baseball etiquette to start another discussion while the older version is still open.

I'm a big believer in etiquette. So, for the sake of argument, why not take all of baseball history going back to the Elysian Fields, and rank the most profound persons, events, and innovations that have affected the game? Changed the game for better or worse, to be exact.

Baseball moves slowly in calm times, sometimes at too pedestrian of a pace and against its best interests and overall logic. Take the vital, long overdue move to racial integration, for example. But the game can turn on a dime, too. Witness the sudden installation of extensive instant replay after embarrassing—HD videoed—umpiring calls in the 2012 postseason were exposed.

For *Baseball's Game Changers*, I decided to throw out a massive number of topics, winnow them down to the top 50, and then rank them based on how dramatically they altered the national pastime. In the process, I moved some game changers up, others down, and designated even more for assignment. I have pounded the keyboard to explain my decisions, and I open up my list for your examination and your disputes. If baseball can't handle a good rhubarb, it can't handle anything.

My Top Five is pretty solid, covering the concepts of how the game is played, who plays it, how it is witnessed by millions and financed, how its stars are paid, and how it keeps corruption at bay. If you want to argue with my quintet of Babe Ruth, Jackie Robinson, television, Marvin Miller, and the Black Sox, by all means hoot and holler. One person's Top Five could very well be someone else's middle of the pack.

Here's the secret: Picking Ruth over Robinson was like splitting hairs. The instant replay decision, after much review, is that Ruth the batsman changed the game instantaneously, like an earthquake, and baseball forever has followed in his image. Robinson broke a color line that should never have existed, but baseball did not fully embrace integration for almost 15 years. Robinson was named National League Most Valuable Player in 1949. The American League could not name an African-American MVP until Elston Howard in 1963. Such was the difference between the leagues in the pace of integration and advancement of stars.

If you want to argue with my quintet of Babe Ruth, Jackie Robinson, television, Marvin Miller, and the Black Sox, by all means hoot and holler.

Television is the mule pulling baseball's financial wagon. Network executives tell their baseball counterparts when to schedule games and how much sleep we'll miss from the late-night telecasts. When in doubt, always follow the money, and the trail always leads back to the TV companies' front offices.

Marvin Miller was likely smart enough to be baseball commissioner. The game, though, could not have been that sensible. Still, baseball is better for Miller's advocacy of players' rights, and both players and owners began making tons more money after his eventful stint as Players Association godfather.

The game threatened to degenerate into a cut above pro wrestling, having been chock full of gambling with reports of fixed games in the early 20th century. The trend came to a head with the Black Sox Scandal. Kenesaw Mountain Landis administered an overdose of castor oil to cleanse its system of corruption. Only the drawn-out Pete Rose affair—and Charlie Hustle never fixed any games—has dovetailed gambling with baseball ever since.

If anything, baseball the game of failure also has a culture of forgiveness. The Black Sox were never reinstated in the real world, but attained redemption on Kevin Costner's diamond-in-the-cornfield in *Field of Dreams*. Rose was at least allowed to participate in 2015 All-Star festivities in his hometown of Cincinnati. Mark McGwire and Barry Bonds, so intertwined with PEDs, have been welcomed back to dispense hitting tips.

Broken-down players consigned to comebacks only via the scriptwriter's keyboard through the cornfield can now do it via Tommy John and arthroscopic surgeries, in a marriage of medicine and baseball. Dr. Frank Jobe's 1974 transplant brainchild on southpaw John gets a particularly high ranking since post-surgery pitchers have no-mileage parts, enabling them to hump up the velocity, the stuff of science fiction a half-century ago.

Ex-catcher Chris Krug (left), whose error led to the only run in Sandy Koufax's 1965 perfect game, meets *Field of Dreams* star Kevin Costner on the set in 1988. Krug's baseball-field company carved out the famous mystical movie diamond from an Iowa cornfield.

After covering baseball in a city whose two teams have rarely possessed bountiful farm systems, I had to put the Branch Rickey innovation of signing and grooming players under a team's control in the Top Ten. The team that skimps on player development will be the one that shortchanges itself on playoff appearances.

I could go on forever. Fortunately, I don't, but I give you enough of a historical repast to sate your appetite for baseball debates. And those of you who look at the photos in books first, well, we have some classic shots. A gorgeous 1960 photo of reigning MVPs Ernie Banks and Nellie Fox together, promoting the onset of baseball color telecasts, is can't-miss stuff. So is a shirtless Bill Veeck in 1981 in all his unabashed glory, returning to the Wrigley Field bleachers he had built 44 years earlier.

Enjoy *Baseball's Game Changers* for a leisurely read or a competitive argument-settling. Baseball can be consumed from many angles, and this book includes a lot of 'em, from 1 to 50.

The Black Sox
Players Fixing Games? Never Again!

The sordid Black Sox affair of 1919–1921 was like a pressure cooker exploding. Gambling and attempts at game-fixing had been intertwined with baseball since touts roamed the sidelines of matches on those green fields in the 1850s.

NO. 5

Once the mess broke out in the open and baseball's version of capital punishment was meted out, baseball never experienced a repeat, nor even hints of the same. Sure, you have the generation-long Pete Rose affair, but Rose was accused of betting on his own team, not actually trying to fix a game in which he played or managed. The specter of throwing games was squarely on Bowie Kuhn's mind as he probed Leo Durocher in the winter of 1969-70, but nothing was ever hung on The Lip.

A proud franchise's standing in a city and some (likely) innocent players were the collateral damage of the Black Sox. So was much-needed progress in the game under the thumb of baseball's first commissioner Kenesaw Mountain Landis, brought in to clean up the mess and centralize authority over the game into one man. Landis's autocratic style retarded progress elsewhere by employing 19th-century sensibilities, most notably opposition to integration, in a sport crying to advance in the 20th century.

"The Black Sox Scandal remains the biggest black eye that organized baseball has ever had, and it ruined the lives and careers of many people involved," said Jacob Pomrenke, web content editor/producer for the Society for American Baseball Research (SABR) and author of *Scandal on the South Side: The 1919 Chicago White Sox*. "That said, it did lead to a permanent (and positive) change in the close relationship between underworld gambling and organized baseball that had flourished during the Dead Ball Era."

As with Jackie Robinson's saga, anyone with even a passing interest in baseball knows about the Black Sox, the nickname for key players from the 1919 Chicago White Sox who were part of baseball's best team, but threw their careers away in a cash-grab deal with gamblers. *Eight Men Out* as a book and 1988 movie was the prime story conduit, while other

The 1919 White Sox assemble for a group portrait.

works have probed all aspects of a game that dovetailed with corruption until the scandal blew up. Redemption from beyond for the guilty formed the basis of *Field of Dreams*, also a 1988 Hollywood production.

The bottom line was that the Black Sox Scandal represented the biggest game-changing single event in baseball history. The scandal essentially made gambling so heinous an offense that signs warning of its consequences are the staple furnishing in all clubhouses. The cleanup resulted in the creation of a commissioner's position that has ruled the game for good and bad ever since.

Baseball likely dodged a bullet in not experiencing a scandal on such a monumental scale before 1919, perhaps because the World Series itself was only 15 years old and wasn't yet established as an event worth fixing. Reports have circulated that the World Series in the war-shortened 1918 season was a prime candidate for tampering. Shady behavior by players and enthusiastic gambling by the hordes of cigar-chomping male fans always seemed too uncomfortably tied to the final game results.

The cleanup resulted in the creation of a commissioner's position that has ruled the game for good and bad ever since.

Ranking the Black Sox as the event rounding out the Top Five of all-time game changers sounds just about right to Rich Lindberg, the White Sox's official historian, author of numerous White Sox and Chicago history books, and advisor to the *Eight Men Out* movie.

"I think the ranking is on point," said Lindberg. "It had a profound impact on the game of baseball because at the very core of the matter was the consequence: the creation of the MLB commissioner, changing the entire course of baseball history. Imagine where we would be today if we still had the old National Commission—a three person gridlock. We might not even have the things we take for granted, e.g., interleague play, the DH, possibly even expansion."

The Black Sox scandal and the appointment of Landis, a longtime colorful federal judge, as grand poobah of baseball might never have occurred if not for key White Sox players' dissatisfaction with their compensation and their relationship with team owner Charles Comiskey. Stereotyped as a cheapskate, Comiskey actually paid market rate for his players by the day's standards. But almost all big leaguers were dissatisfied with salaries that still put them way above workingmen's status in the early 1900s. A scandal required the right kind of scoundrel-like players such as ringleader Chick Gandil consorting with seemingly small-timers like Bill Burns and Sport Sullivan in a plot that might have been branded a wacky comedy if the results weren't so tragic for so many individuals and the White Sox as a franchise.

Gandil, hitter extraordinaire "Shoeless Joe" Jackson, Sox ace Eddie Cicotte, regulars Happy Felsch and Swede Risberg, backup Fred McMullin, and southpaw starter Lefty Williams were squarely in on the attempted fix. Sox third baseman Buck Weaver abstained from the plot, yet had knowledge of the nefarious skulking about. In the time-honored tradition of baseball, Weaver refused to tattle on his teammates.

Too many people tried to look the other way as hints of the plot leaked out while the favored Sox were upset by the Cincinnati Reds in the 1919 World Series. The scandal bubbled under the surface as the 1920 season entered the home stretch with the Sox in contention for the AL pennant. Yet it was the crosstown Cubs who ultimately triggered the Black Sox investigation.

On August 31, 1920, Cubs president William L. Veeck caught wind of an apparent plot to fix the game with the Phillies at Cubs Park. Taking quick action to bar players connected with the fix, Veeck appealed to newspapers for help in further exposing the plot. But instead of investigating the Cubs situation, a Cook County grand jury instead turned its attention to the long-rumored White Sox scandal.

The plotters and Weaver were put on trial in Chicago to answer for the fraud. Their eventual "not guilty" verdict a year later was likely a hometown call. But the day after their acquittal, Landis issued a sweeping ban of all the clearly guilty players plus Weaver, the latter condemned due to guilt by association. Landis thus extended the imperious nature of his former courtroom to the mass ban. He would have his ears to the rails on gambling the rest of his career, banning 11 more players and carefully scrutinizing Rogers Hornsby's indebtedness from betting on the horses. His zealotry squeezed the age-old problem of gambling clear out of baseball.

"The Black Sox Scandal for the most part put a stop to the pernicious influence of gambling on the game," said Lindberg, "and made a lot of players think twice about consorting with gamblers."

Memories of the scandal have forever hovered over baseball. Exactly a half-century later, Landis successor four-times-removed Kuhn shuddered with nightmares of Black Sox II when Durocher's handling of his first-place Cubs lineup during a crucial pennant-race series in Shea Stadium on September 8-9, 1969, drew red flags. A rumor was floated that Durocher made questionable moves against the on-charging Mets to settle a $50,000 gambling debt. With The Lip's track record of association with fast-crowd, unsavory types, and a season ban in 1947, Kuhn launched a secret probe of the game's most disliked manager. Chicago sports columnist Rick Talley—Durocher's prime critic—caught wind of the investigation, but Kuhn asked him to sit on the news for the good of baseball. Other investigative bodies also checked on Durocher. Nothing was proven and his record stayed clean through his Hall of Fame induction in 1991.

Pete Rose's lifetime ban by commissioner Bart Giamatti in 1989 still resonates today. "Charlie Hustle" at least had enough respect for the game to not fix it. But his compulsive personality, whether running out a walk or using his superior sports knowledge to gamble, simply overwhelmed his entire being. In 2015, Rose still remained ineligible for a formal baseball job or election to the Hall of Fame.

Third baseman Buck Weaver had knowledge of the Black Sox fix discussions, but was banned for life because he did not report the plot to Charles Comiskey.

The dark post–Black Sox side of Landis, who had been boosted for the commissioner's job by original anti-gambling man Veeck and his allies, was his autocratic, iron-hand nature made even worse by traditionalism. Landis was hardly the progressive the game needed to complement the anti-gambling actions. Dramatic changes, such as Branch Rickey's farm system, were usually viewed unfavorably by Landis. He did not immediately recognize new revenue opportunities, such as network radio rights. Worst was his opposition to integration of baseball, clouded by platitudes and sanctimony.

Landis gutted Comiskey's team with his wholesale ban of most of the key players. The White Sox, the AL's pre-eminent team in the pre–Babe Ruth/Yankees era, were thrown back to the dark ages. They did not return to consistent contention until 1951. But the impact of being consigned to second-fiddle status to the Cubs in Chicago was much longer lasting.

"The scandal definitely tilted the scales of power and prominence from the Sox to the Cubs in fan popularity," Lindberg said. "It didn't happen overnight, but I would say that after 1929, and the Cubs' World Series appearance (with superstars Hornsby and Hack Wilson) it was a fait accompli.

"In many respects the aftershocks of the scandal reverberate still today. Who knows how many pennants that Black Sox team might have won in the 1920s? Or if Charles Comiskey's health might not have been imperiled as it was (he died in 1931) by this tragedy? A fully competent Comiskey might have made the right rebuilding moves to have kept the Sox in the pennant chase well into the 1930s."

Landis affixed a one-size-fits-all suspension to Weaver, who never had any intention of taking cash to get in on the fix. Yet Landis expected him to play snitch, against all baseball customs, when he proclaimed, "No player that sits in a conference with a bunch of crooked players and gamblers where the ways and means of throwing games are planned and discussed and does not promptly tell his club about it, will ever play professional baseball." The banning of Weaver may have had an even more lasting effect on heading off gambling scandals before they could get out of the talking stage than casting out Weaver's crooked teammates, according to Dr. David Fletcher. Also founder of the Chicago Baseball Museum, Fletcher represents the Weaver estate and started the ClearBuck.com campaign in 2003 to get the late third baseman's ban lifted.

"Landis' harsh treatment of Weaver ranks as the most important baseball decision Landis or any future commissioner ever issued," said Fletcher. "Weaver had admitted to Landis in December 1921 he had participated in two meetings with the other Black Sox conspirators before the World Series but rejected taking part in the plot."

After Landis's lifetime ban of Weaver, only two new attempts at game-fixing took place: Shufflin' Phil Douglas in 1922 and the O'Connell-Dolan affair in 1924. In both cases, the players approached to throw games instantly turned in the seducing game-fixers, who ended up getting banned from baseball.

"Weaver's integrity to not snitch on his teammates for fixing the 1919 World Series forever changed baseball," said Fletcher.

The game required the strongest kind of medicine, the type that unfortunately claims victims as it works its cure.

Like a "wrong man" victim in a Hitchcock movie, Weaver spent the rest of his life trying to exonerate himself and be reinstated. His fight was carried on by his family long after his 1956 death. In 2015, Weaver niece Patricia Anderson, 88, and other kin petitioned new commissioner Rob Manfred for Weaver's reinstatement. Manfred replied to Fletcher on July 20, 2015 that available evidence supported Weaver's knowledge of the fixing plot, and thus he would not reinstate him.

Apparently no player other than Rose has crossed the line since Landis's era. Spitballs, PEDs, and corked bats became the reigning scandals in the near-century since the Black Sox. But baseball must continue to be vigilant to avoid a recurrence of that convulsive Warren Harding–era game changer.

After Landis's lifetime ban of Weaver, only two new attempts at game-fixing took place: Shufflin' Phil Douglas in 1922 and the O'Connell-Dolan affair in 1924.

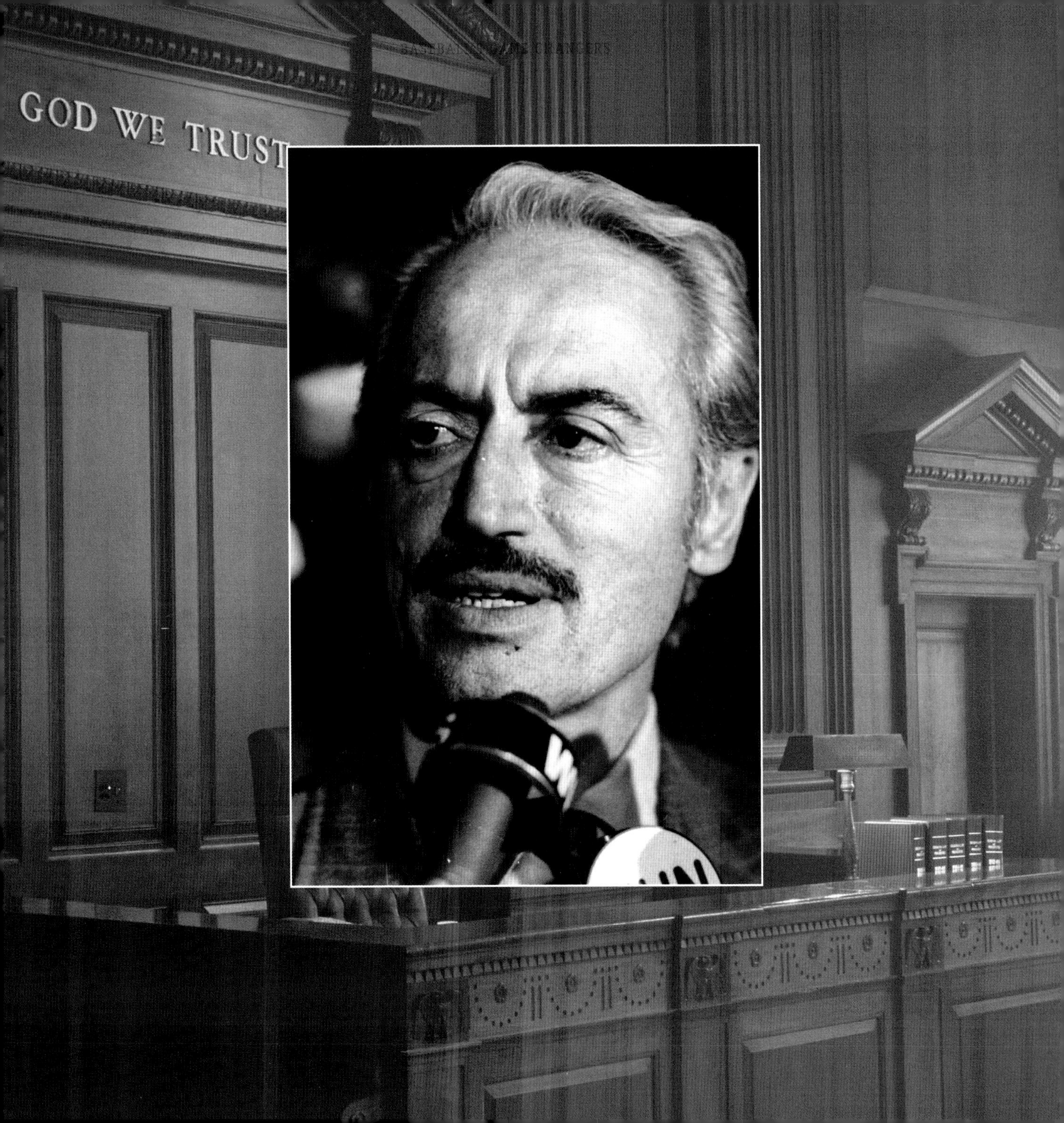
GOD WE TRUST

Marvin Miller

The Man Who Outsmarted Baseball's Hidebound Establishment

Nearly five decades after major leaguers began amassing workplace rights, baseball's need for an organized body of players and a learned advocate for players' rights was still being acknowledged by even the most conservative of baseball's establishment.

One day in the early 2000s, a dual history lesson was exchanged beside the tiny salad bar in the Wrigley Field pressbox dining room. Cubs president Andy MacPhail was prepping his lunch when he was informed of a bizarre occurrence from the ivy-encrusted ballpark's not-so-distant past. On the Friday through Monday of the Labor Day weekend in 1967, the Cubs had played four consecutive doubleheaders—the first three with the Mets necessitated by rainouts, and the final a regularly scheduled holiday twinbill with the Dodgers. MacPhail was told not only about the overload of games, but also how amoral Cubs manager Leo Durocher started the same lineup, including catcher Randy Hundley and 36-year-old creaky-kneed Ernie Banks, in seven out of the eight contests.

A third-generation baseball executive, MacPhail did not pause with his reaction.

"That's why you needed the Players Association," he said.

And that's why, even as Durocher's chain-gang approach to lineups proved the Cubs' undoing two years later, a soft-spoken gentleman—almost too scholarly for baseball—was taking steps to give the players the same basic rights other workers in the US economy had long enjoyed. Within the next decade, Marvin Miller radically changed the game as the smartest man in baseball, checkmating the owners and their legal representatives with patience, prudence, and an inside-out knowledge of labor law. By the time he retired in 1982, this former steelworkers union economist had transformed the Players Association into the most powerful union in the country while helping enrich owners even further despite their fight against Miller and the players every step of the way. In his 16 years as executive director, the

Marvin turned the Players Association into the country's most powerful union.

average player's annual salary rose from $19,000 to $326,000, according to published salary surveys. "Marvin Miller, along with Babe Ruth and Jackie Robinson, is one of the two or three most important men in baseball history," former Dodgers and Yankees broadcast sage Red Barber said in 1992.

When Miller died at 95 in 2012, former commissioner Fay Vincent also placed Miller in the exalted class of baseball history. "I think he's the most important baseball figure of the last 50 years," Vincent said. "He changed not just the sport but the business of the sport permanently, and he truly emancipated the baseball player—and in the process all professional athletes."

Long before Greg Maddux became known as the brainiest man in the game with just a high school education, Miller's towering intellectualism beat the owners at every turn. Less than a handful of Miller's management negotiating opponents—MacPhail's father Lee MacPhail being one—proved even worthy of sitting at the same bargaining table.

Formerly a fractious group with a thin layer of decently compensated superstars topping the underpaid masses, the players learned from Miller their strength came in numbers and a united front. Rather than conducting economics and law lectures that would put the most rabbit-eared player to sleep, Miller taught the Players Association members to ask questions for themselves. "The way he laid it out, he didn't make it complicated," said ex–third baseman Bill Melton, the American League's 1971 home-run champ with the White Sox. "We were a bunch of stupid baseball players trying to hit hanging curveballs in spring training. He was very fluent in explaining to a lot of players who didn't want to listen to that stuff."

Miller's savvy benefited not only players, but also coaches and managers. The appreciation echoes through the decades, even after some of those players ended up in front-office ranks.

On Marvin Miller's Motivation

"He was the backbone of the union. When he spoke, you knew honesty was coming out of his mouth on behalf of the players. I don't think he intentionally looked at it and said, 'Screw these owners.' He said let's equal these playing fields." —*Hall of Fame pitcher Bert Blyleven*

SPITBALLING

"A two-edged sword for me," longtime baseball executive Dallas Green, a Phillies and Senators pitcher in the pre-Miller days, said of his long-term impact. "I played and managed [Phillies, Yankees, Mets], so I'm a beneficiary of the health program, and the pension program that was set up as a result of it. As a [Cubs] GM, it was tough to deal with all the rules and regulations that have come as a result of the strength of the Players Association."

Growing up a Dodgers fan in Brooklyn, Miller employed his own love of the game to transform its basic financial and competitive structure. Open to a job change after a long tenure with the steelworkers in 1965, Miller took over a toothless organization that was hardly better than a company union. They thought any big name might help them, so Miller had to quash a misguided effort to hire Richard Nixon, hardly a union man, as Players Association counsel.

Miller also had to deal with stubborn racism that beset the game. In a company union pre-Miller, a black man apparently could not represent his teammates.

By the time he retired in 1982, this former steelworkers union economist had transformed the Players Association into the most powerful union in the country.

"We had a meeting to elect a player rep," George Altman, the Cubs' first regular African-American outfielder, recalled of an early 1960s gathering. "They were trying to get Ernie [Banks] to run. I decided to run, and I thought I had some pretty good votes. Suddenly someone came down [from the front office] and they said they wanted Bob Will [a white outfielder] to be the player rep. That was that."

Miller first had to win over reluctant players, then educate them about basic workplace rights that should have long been attainable. The players thought they had little leverage under the reserve clause and thus never employed a legal advocate who could have challenged its outwardly binding concepts. Even stellar production did not assure fair compensation by owners, who often viewed themselves as paternalistic.

The poster boy for such conditions may have been Stan Musial. Having established himself with the Cardinals and settled in the St. Louis area with business interests, Musial did not get a pay raise over the seven years after the then-lucrative $75,000 deal, with a $5,000 attendance clause, that he signed with owner Fred Saigh for the 1951 season. In the ensuing period, he won three batting titles (to add to his previous four crowns) and an RBI title. Finally, successor St. Louis owner Gussie Busch made Musial the highest-paid National League player with a $100,000 contract after his seventh batting crown (.351) in 1957.

But Musial was such a man of principle that he asked for a pay cut after hitting .255 in 1959. Busch gladly obliged, slashing Musial's pay to $80,000. The Cardinals continued to cut his pay down to $65,000 for 1962, when he batted .330. Busch declined to cut his pay for his final season in 1963.

How star players were treated served as a guidebook for management's treatment of all their players. Blyleven noticed a Musial-like situation with flinty Twins owner Calvin Griffith never paying Hall of Fame Twins slugger Harmon Killebrew anywhere near his true worth as a top runs producer, franchise icon, and pillar of the community. Killebrew topped out at $115,000 in 1971-72.

"Harmon went through that," he said. "Harmon basically was such a great gentleman. Whatever Calvin offered him, well, Harmon said if that's what you think I'm worth, I'll take that. That hurt Tony Oliva and Rod Carew, because nobody got paid more than Harmon. Calvin used that to his advantage."

The players were simply beaten down over the years. Miller found the minimum salary, the only pay level ever legislated in the game, then and now, was just $6,000 in the mid-1960s. The minimum had risen just $1,000 in two decades. Amassing a few years' experience did not necessarily lift a player's paycheck into the upper middle class. In 1967, the median salary was just $17,000. More than 40 percent of players earned $12,000 or less. No wonder the players of that era could relate well to the sportswriters who covered them—their pay was in the same ballpark.

An owner's word wasn't always trustworthy, as Blyleven found out one offseason negotiating with the nickel-biting Griffith.

"He said if you win 15 or more games, I'll give you a $2,000 bonus," Blyleven said. "He had to write it on a piece of paper. I won 16. I kept the piece of paper. He denied ever signing that thing. He wouldn't put that in the contract. I had to show him that paper, so thank God I kept it."

One owner's effort to set a salary standard was met with lifted eyebrows elsewhere. As part of his quirky thread of ownership, the Cubs' Phil Wrigley set a scale of $15,000 for starting pitchers in 1958, according to then-budding author Jim Brosnan. Imagine the shock of Cardinals GM Bing Devine, who helped supervise Musial's elongated pay freeze, when he traded for Brosnan early in the '58 season and found himself stuck with the $15-K contract for the rest of the year. By the time Brosnan moved on to Cincinnati, he had penned *The Long Season* and *Pennant Race*, and was in the home stretch of his career in 1962. And he had crept all the way to $28,000.

As Miller became established as executive director going into the 1970s, he negotiated a $13,500 minimum and impartial grievance arbitration, among other modest improvements. The 1968 collective bargaining agreement had stood as the first in any pro sport. Attempts to change the hated reserve-clause system that seemingly bound players to their teams into perpetuity went nowhere. Miller adopted a careful, go-slow approach to the reserve system that paid off years later.

Then-commissioner Bowie Kuhn believed Miller wanted to provoke a strike to kick off the 1972 season. The issue at hand? The owners' firm stand on increasing pension benefits. But as the most experienced official in labor relations in the entire process, Miller always believed a strike was the absolute last resort. And only six years into his tenure, Miller was not rock-solid confident about his members' resolve.

"The last thing I expected in 1972 was a strike. It really caught me unawares . . . The very last thing I wanted at that time was a strike; the truth is that I wasn't sure we were strong enough," Miller wrote in his 1991 autobiography *A Whole Different Ball Game: The Sport and Business of Baseball*. The players eventually walked out in pro sports' first-ever strike, wiping out the season's first seven or eight games.

But the owners compromised to end the work stoppage, the first of an unbroken string of Miller victories. Soon the game had salary arbitration, followed by the end of the reserve clause, thanks to arbitrator Peter Seitz's ruling in Andy Messersmith's and Dave McNally's bids for free agency late in 1975. But, licking their wounds over their loss of ironclad control—while at the same time granting selective lucrative contracts—the owners allowed labor relations to worsen by the dawn of the 1980s. Miller unfortunately had to shepherd the players through a nearly two-month-long strike that fractured the 1981 campaign and forced Kuhn and Co. to create first and second halves of the season.

The players eventually walked out in pro sports' first-ever strike, wiping out the season's first seven or eight games.

Again, the players held firm thanks to Miller's organizing and educational skills. He retired in 1982, leaving deputy Don Fehr to navigate the Players Association through even stormier seas—the owners' collusion of 1986-87 and the nearly catastrophic strike of 1994-95 that wiped out a World Series for the first time in history.

Eventually, both sides learned they had nothing to gain, and almost everything to lose, from continued conflict. The 2002 collective bargaining agreement was the first achieved—barely—without any kind of labor stoppage. Successive CBAs were negotiated in near-secret to avoid vitriolic public comments. One hot-button issue remained throughout Miller's long life—lack of inclusion in Hall of Fame voting. "Definitely," Blyleven said of Miller's place in Cooperstown. "He changed the game. These players today, I bet you 90 percent of them don't know who Marvin is.

"I wish they did, because he changed the game."

Television
Bulging Baseball Coffers Thanks to an Up-Close-and-Personal Medium

At different junctures, baseball—the nation's oldest team sport—and television—its most influential medium—have held a dominant position over the other. Baseball came first, becoming America's national pastime by the turn of the 20th century. Television burst on the scene in the middle of that 100-year span to quickly ally itself with baseball. Seemingly, it was a dog-and-tail situation. Did the tail wag the dog? Who controlled whom?

NO.

After all, television bestowed the first billion—*billion*, remember—dollar deal on the game through the 1983 network contract with Major League Baseball, dramatically stuffing the coffers of owners and boosting player salaries for the first time into the multi-millions. Television moved the World Series from glorious fall-colors daytime play to often-frigid 8:30 p.m. (Eastern Time) first pitches stretching to Halloween, and sometimes beyond. Shadows engulfed 5:00 p.m. gametimes on the West Coast.

There's much more. The need for profit lengthened each game, as the one-minute commercial breaks of a half-century ago became the two-and-a-half minutes standard today. And within the last decade, the former in-game sanctity of the dugout has been invaded by mandated live and taped comments by microphoned managers and players while all-seeing cameras record every reaction on the bench.

Two savvy media *artistes* who employ the latest in video technology to tell their Emmy Award–winning stories, while fully understanding the politics and rhythms of baseball from cumulative decades of working the game, are as competent as any other pundits to analyze the baseball versus television struggle for dominance.

"I'm going to say it's both," said Comcast SportsNet Chicago senior producer Sarah Lauch. "Especially the way we do things and how the team and we are partners. Obviously

Reigning 1959 MVPs Ernie Banks of the Cubs and Nellie Fox of the White Sox join WGN broadcaster Jack Brickhouse around an RCA TK-41.

people love the game and want to see the game. TV now brings the game to people from 500 different angles. I think it cuts both ways."

"I do think there are times when we wag their tail," fellow senior producer Ryan McGuffey said. "I think there's times when television controls baseball and baseball controls television. There are times when baseball needs television to wag the tail. When television thinks they're in charge, baseball kind of brings you back to reality, and takes back control. And once they get control again, they need TV . . . It's the handing off of a baton.

"They both need each other to survive."

Whatever the tilt and pull of their relationship, baseball and television have been an inseparable pair since TV stations signed on in many of the original 10 markets—five of which were hosting two or more teams—confined to the northeastern quarter of the country. During an overall boom in baseball attendance after World War II, fans in New York, Chicago, Philadelphia, and Boston doubled their pleasure with virtually all home games of their teams televised. In an era of much lower revenues, teams paid bills with the extra $75,000 or $100,000 in annual TV rights. The fledgling stations, not yet conveying a full day's worth of network shows, needed blocs of high-quality programming to fill their schedules. Baseball attracted more viewers as families purchased their first TV sets. Meanwhile, the game helped stations lure bread-and-butter advertisers for the male demographic, like companies shilling beer, gasoline, and cigarettes.

> **Whatever the tilt and pull of their relationship, baseball and television have been an inseparable pair since TV stations signed on in many of the original 10 markets.**

In no other city did the home-bound fan prosper as much as Chicago, with the Cubs. Despite his various mistakes, owner Philip K. Wrigley concocted one master stroke of promotion that proved way ahead of his time and reverberates to this day.

Having learned the value of broadcast exposure from his late father, William Wrigley Jr., the gum magnate swung his namesake ballpark's gates wide open for video cameras. By 1949, three of the four stations on the air in Chicago showed all Cubs home games simultaneously. Wrigley spent $100,000 to construct new vantage points for cameras and TV crews while foregoing formal rights fees. Each of the stations—WGN, WBKB, and ABC-owned WENR—merely had to pay a $5,000 "construction" fee.

By the time WGN acquired exclusive Cubs TV rights in 1952, the picture-tube habit had formed with the mass audience. Children ran home from school to catch the final few innings of the all-daytime schedule, ensuring interest for the future when they had disposable income for ticket-buying. Wrigley charged under-market rights fees so WGN was assured an annual profit televising the stumblebum Cubs. Wrigley Field may have hosted fewer than 600 fans on three occasions during lost September weekdays in 1962, 1965, and 1966, but the fans were no farther away than their TV sets. For the better part of four decades starting in the early 1950s, the bounty of TV exposure in Chicago and to a slightly lesser extent New York stood out as an exception.

Stung by declining attendance that reversed the late 1940s boom and displaying the eventually discredited stance about TV exposure hurting the gate, the majority of owners soon cut the number of telecasts, particularly home games. Most extreme was owner Lou Perini's total ban on TV coverage of his Braves—overreacting to a sharp drop in attendance at Braves Field in the years after the 1948 pennant—when he moved from Boston to Milwaukee. Walter O'Malley and Horace Stoneham totally reversed course, leading the pack of contra-Wrigley owners on televised exposure, when they moved their Dodgers and Giants, respectively, to Los Angeles and San Francisco in late 1957. All Dodgers and Giants home games, and 25 Brooklyn road games, had been televised in the previous three seasons. Now, amid the car culture–oriented West Coast, O'Malley and Stoneham put their teams on a starvation TV diet of only the road games from each other's ballparks. Early network game-of-the-week deals hardly expanded the weekly TV ration. Dizzy Dean and his fractured syntax was a staple of CBS's Saturday and Sunday coverage for a decade starting in 1955, but his and competing NBC telecasts with Leo Durocher and Lindsey Nelson were blacked out in big-league markets to protect the live gate and competing local telecasts. So if a fan happened to live in a city other than New York and Chicago, he was often out of luck for televised baseball many spring and summer weekends. One team really shot itself in its foot, limiting exposure and slowing expansion of its fan base with ill-advised broadcasting strategies. The White Sox shared the high profile on WGN with the Cubs from 1948 on, but barred telecasts of its 22 or 23 annual night games at old Comiskey Park until the mid-1960s. Then, Sox owner Arthur Allyn traded short-term gain for long-term problems to bolt WGN for UHF upstart WFLD starting with the 1968 season.

Although the million-dollar deal kept the Sox afloat through some very lean years, the switch to a station that at least half the Chicago market could not receive—UHF tuners were only mandatory starting with 1964 set models—hurt the fan base. The mistake on prematurely switching games to a hard-to-receive outlet was repeated in 1982, when the Sox and three other Chicago pro franchises began SportsVision, a $20 a month subscription TV service requiring a converter box to descramble the signal. Problem was, Chicago-area fans were not yet used to paying for TV as very little of the region had been cabled. Going up against the Cubs' free broadcast colossus on WGN, the Sox were locked into second-team status

On the First Commercials Aired on Televised Baseball

"They put the camera on me, and I held up a box of Wheaties and poured them in a bowl. I took a banana and a knife, and I sliced the banana onto the Wheaties. Then I poured in some milk and said, 'That's the Breakfast of Champions.'" —*Hall of Fame announcer Red Barber, who called baseball's first televised game*

SPITBALLING

in the market due to the decreased exposure on SportsVision, which eventually morphed into a basic-cable channel.

The rights totals were modest by 21st-century standards. A six-year World Series deal starting in 1950, inaugurating NBC's longtime coverage, netted $6 million. In 1957, the World Series and All-Star Game generated $3.2 million, while the CBS Game of the Week spewed forth $1.26 million to participating teams. Meanwhile, local rights were worth $4.84 million.

ABC's 1965 Game of the Week deal was the first that shared revenue with all teams, at $300,000 each. But the telecasts, featuring another color-line breaking by announcer Jackie Robinson, were low-rated even though they were the first Saturday games beamed into all big-league markets. NBC finally won exclusivity for both the Saturday telecasts and the World Series/All-Star Game with a $30.6 million deal taking effect in 1966. The first steps into network prime-time baseball were part of the deal: three holiday games and the All-Star Game.

NBC was the signature network for baseball through 1976, when ABC joined the package with Monday Night telecasts and sharing the World Series, League Championship Series, and All-Star Game. By now the payoff was $92.8 million, just in time to pay the first crop of free agents.

Soon a trio of superstations—TBS, WGN, and WWOR—and the 1979-founded ESPN generated additional dollars and exposure to complement the old-style over-the-air telecast as cable proliferated in the 1980s. The network deal was $185 million from 1980 to 1983 as Nolan Ryan of the Astros became the game's first $1 million per year player. Upon expiration of this deal, NBC and ABC re-upped for $1.2 billion over six years. Each big-league franchise got a $7.7 million cut of the new windfall, some $500,000 more than the average team payroll.

CBS practically jumped the shark by paying $1.1 billion by itself for a five-year, all-encompassing deal from 1990 to 1994. The erstwhile "Tiffany Network" shelled out more for less, televising just 16 Saturday Game of the Weeks. Meanwhile, ESPN jumped in by paying out $400 million for a four-year deal as Major League Baseball calculated to shift more primetime games to cable. Baseball owners spent the TV money practically as soon as it came into their coffers, bloating their payrolls, then asking the players for relief via a salary cap and other major givebacks that did not fly. As a result, the game suffered its most devastating strike in 1994-95 while CBS licked its wounds with $500 million of losses from its overambitious deal.

The money and salaries continue to skyrocket even though baseball long ceded its primacy to pro football. Postseason baseball is often scheduled around NFL and college games, and rarely slotted for early Saturday or Sunday afternoon as when the League Championship Series was inaugurated in 1969.

ABC's 1965 Game of the Week deal was the first that shared revenue with all teams, at $300,000 each.

A kind of full cycle has been reached. After its financial empowerment of baseball and decades of technical advances, television has turned each ballpark into a major production studio. Camera placements, up-close-and-personal views of the dugout and home-run trots, and HD picture clarity that were science fiction in 1967 are daily expectations of the home-bound viewer. To some, they surpass the ballpark experience.

Maybe the money and the technology are too much of a good thing. Owners have spent most of their TV dollars on player payroll. Now, they must recoup some of that money and ensure profits. Thus the $50 reserved bleacher seat and $8 hot dogs and beer, making the in-game experience, once accessible and affordable, almost a relic of the past.

Today there are several-times-daily televised baseball games, more than making up for 1950s-originated TV scarcity, with broadcasts originating from a cornucopia of sources—over-the-air local stations, Fox, ESPN, TBS, regional sports networks, and the MLB Network.

In 2012, a Chicago Blackhawks official greeted a reporter at the United Center's press gate to straighten out a credential request. "I know you came here to work," said the sympathetic gent who immediately granted admission. "Otherwise, it's just better to stay home and watch it on the big screen." Documentarians/storytellers Lauch and McGuffey have picked up on this stark fact. "That's why teams are getting more inventive about getting you to the game," McGuffey said. "Television makes it easier to watch. As a father myself, it makes it easier to say, 'Let's keep $130 or $140 in my pocket and have a baseball experience at home.'"

A Fawcett Publication

NO. 5

Jackie Robinson

10¢

Special!

INSIDE THE
DODGER TRAINING
CAMP!

READ

ROOKIE ON TRIAL!

Jackie Robinson
Baseball's Gift to a Changing Society

Jackie Robinson easily could be ranked the top game changer in baseball.

You could flip a coin with Babe Ruth, the actual top man. An even more accurate ranking than number two could be "1-A." Robinson opened up a talent pool that truly makes baseball a game representing all, ensuring that if a man could play, he could have a job. And he represented the first step in modernizing a sport that even at mid-20th century was simply continuing a 1900-vintage manner of operation.

Ruth gets the nod because his two-decade-long career dramatically changed the style of baseball, generating numbers by which much of the statistical guts of the game are measured. And his outsized personality strode like a colossus above all sports.

Robinson was a good-to-great ballplayer in his own right, but not Ruth-ian in achievement or colorful persona. Yet he had a huge impact. Robinson meant more for society in general than for baseball itself. His major league debut became a "Point A" for the as-yet-unfulfilled drive for a true American meritocracy.

Jim Crow governed the South in 1947 as if the region had negotiated a deal to end the Civil War rather than surrendering outright. But the remainder of the United States had de facto segregation—held firm by custom and by fear. African Americans could vote north of the Mason-Dixon Line, but they largely had to exist within their own communities with the exception of some public accommodations, government jobs, and limited private industry. Nothing, however, started really moving until Branch Rickey, plotting Robinson's debut on multiple levels, finessed his signing, minor-league debut in tolerant Montreal, and break-in amid team turmoil on the Dodgers and Cardinals. Robinson was a rare personality for the era in integrating a major American institution.

Jackie Robinson was bombarded with offers of endorsements and appearances, and even comic book treatment.

Any baseball fan knows how Robinson ran the gauntlet of prejudice and ignorance. But despite the hatred Robinson endured, he was also an instant celebrity whom some suggest became the most famous American on this side of President Harry S Truman in 1947. Media coverage at the time suggests how famous he became in a very short time. The staid *New York Times* took full note of Robinson's debut. The night after his first game, a reporter for the baseball establishment–backing *Sporting News* booked time for a feature-length interview with Robinson in his Brooklyn apartment. Rachel Robinson had gone out during the writer's visit, leaving the player and infant son Jackie Robinson Jr. as the backdrop for the story.

Robinson quickly became baseball's greatest-ever one-season gate attraction as black fans streamed into ballparks in unprecedented numbers. Rickey the businessman, who seemingly knew of every nickel of cash flow, had shrewdly anticipated this aspect of the color line's shattering. The Dodgers drew a record 1.8 million fans to Ebbets Field. However, Robinson's appeal was never more in evidence than on May 18, 1947, at Wrigley Field. The Dodgers' first visit to Chicago, on a Sunday, drew a regular-season-record paying crowd of 47,101, some 10,000 more than capacity. Only World Series games in 1929 and 1932, and a June 27, 1930 Ladies Day crowd of 51,556, packed more fans into the Friendly Confines.

Robinson quickly became baseball's greatest-ever one-season gate attraction as black fans streamed into ballparks in unprecedented numbers.

Tens of thousands of African-American fans made their first trip to the all-white North Side to witness Robinson. Another attendee at the game was future Pulitzer Prize–winning columnist Mike Royko, then a 15-year-old who walked by his estimate "five to six" miles to Wrigley Field to save on streetcar fare.

In his October 25, 1972, *Chicago Daily News* column, on the day Robinson passed away at 53, Royko described the attitude of the baseball fans in his all-white, ethnic neighborhood toward the newcomer: "Most of the things they said, I didn't understand, although it all sounded terrible. But could one man bring such ruin?"

From his standing-room vantage point in back of the lower-deck grandstand, Royko then painted the picture of the mass of African-American fans, dressed as if they were witnessing a Second Coming at Wrigley Field: "They had on church clothes and funeral clothes: suits, white shirts, ties, gleaming shoes, and straw hats. I've never seen so many straw hats."

During the game, Royko alluded to a "hometown hero" trying to go out of his way to step on first baseman Robinson's foot as the former hit the bag. He was too nice to name Phil Cavarretta, the MVP of the National League in 1945 who as Cubs manager six years later would break in Ernie Banks and Gene Baker as the team's first two black players.

At one point Robinson sliced a foul ball into the grandstands, skipping over outstretched hands until it ended up in the grasp of . . . Royko himself. A black fan who had spent the game standing next to Royko and his buddy asked him, "Would you consider selling that?" Royko was first inclined to say no.

"I'll give you ten dollars for it," he said.

"Ten dollars," Royko wrote. "I couldn't believe it. I didn't know what ten dollars could buy because I'd never had that much money. But I knew that a lot of men in the neighborhood considered sixty dollars a week to be good pay.

"I handed it to him, and he paid me with ten $1 bills.

"When I left the ball park, with that much money in my pocket, I was sure that Jackie Robinson wasn't bad for the game."

The majority of fans who were not tossing epithets toward Robinson wanted to get close to him. By mid-season, the Dodgers had received around 3,000 requests for speeches, personal appearances, and endorsements for their unique rookie. At that point, Rickey cut off the requests, claiming Robinson would wear out physically trying to even handle a fraction of the total.

He would appear before even more people when the Dodgers played the Yankees in the first televised World Series in October 1947. The first mass audience for a TV program tuned in mostly in bars and other public venues in New York, Albany, Philadelphia, and Washington, DC.

Robinson's celebrity, and his class under duress, set things in motion. Truman became the first president to address the NAACP, at the Lincoln Memorial in 1947. The following year, Truman ordered the desegregation of the armed forces. "Dixiecrats" splintered from the Democratic Party and its civil rights proclivities in 1948, running South Carolina's Strom

On "Patience" in the Fight for Civil Rights

"I was sitting in the audience at the Summit Meeting of Negro Leaders yesterday when you said we must have patience. On hearing you say this, I felt like standing up and saying, 'Oh no! Not again.'" —*from a letter by Jackie Robinson to President Dwight D. Eisenhower, May 13, 1958*

SPITBALLING

Thurmond as a third-party candidate opposing Truman. Within six years, the Supreme Court outlawed segregated schools in *Brown v. Board of Education*. Civil rights were now on the front burner of the American agenda.

Robinson waited until after the 1947 season to really cash in on major-league stardom. In his own memoirs, he described how he and his traveling party ate like pigs on the appearance circuit. Robinson arrived in spring training 1948 some 30 pounds overweight. His numbers dipped somewhat compared to his Rookie of the Year season.

But he rebounded with a vengeance in 1949. Serving frequently as the Dodgers' cleanup hitter, he amassed one of the best all-around seasons of the era with a league-leading .342 average and 37 stolen bases along with 16 homers, 124 RBIs, 203 hits, and 122 runs scored. He was an easy Most Valuable Player choice. Robinson went on to hit at least .308 in each of the next five years.

The Robinson experiment was a smashing success both on and off the field. But contrary to perception, his feats did not lead to an immediate rush to integrate rosters. Only two other teams did so in 1947: the Bill Veeck–owned Indians with Larry Doby breaking the American League color line on July 5 in Chicago, and the increasingly desperate St. Louis Browns soon afterward with Hank Thompson and Willard Brown, who combined for just 48 games. No other teams integrated in 1948, and only the New York Giants crossed the line for the first time with Monte Irvin in 1949. Rickey's migration to the Pittsburgh Pirates in 1951 did not mean immediate integration for that team. Infielder Curt Roberts was the Buccos' first African-American player in 1954.

As the color line fell haltingly team by team, black players and the first wave of Latino players found themselves almost an island unto themselves, as Roberto Clemente experienced on the mid-1950s Pirates. The Cubs' Baker had to cool his heels playing shortstop four straight years at Triple-A Los Angeles while the less talented Roy Smalley Sr. and Tommy Brown held down the position in Chicago. He did not get the call until the Cubs signed Ernie Banks from the Negro League Kansas City Monarchs in September 1953. The pair thus could serve as road roommates.

The unwritten rule that no team could field a majority African-American lineup lasted until the start of the 1956 season with the Dodgers and the Cubs, of all teams, breaking the numbers barrier. In Brooklyn ace Don Newcombe's first start on April 17, the regulars included third baseman Robinson, catcher Roy Campanella, left fielder Junior Gilliam, and rookie second baseman Charlie Neal. Several days later, Chicago's Sam "Toothpick" Jones took the mound backed by shortstop Banks, second baseman Baker, left fielder Irvin, and rookie center fielder Solly Drake. At that point, three big-league teams still had not integrated.

Smoothing the entrance for each black National League player was Robinson himself. Banks and others recalled how the venerated star dispensed sage advice for young players of color about how to handle big-league life. Rules of the day prohibited fraternization between teams on the field. But Robinson realized he had to shepherd this brotherhood through tough times.

While eventually up to 27 percent of big leaguers were African Americans in the 1970s and a black manager no longer was a novelty by the 1990s, a glass ceiling of sorts still exists in the game. Only a smattering of black general managers have been hired, while lords-of-the-realm ranks have yet to welcome an African-American majority owner.

Thus the post–playing career baseball opportunities for Robinson were slim. He never had a formal connection to baseball the rest of his life except for his 1962 induction into the Hall of Fame, and a second color line he broke— one for which he still receives little credit. ABC Sports impresario Roone Arledge hired Robinson as color analyst for the network's one-season, poorly rated Saturday *Game of the Week* in 1965. Robinson was the first African American to serve as a network sports announcer. When NBC obtained the weekly network TV rights in 1966, Pee Wee Reese—Dizzy Dean's old partner—was brought back. No black baseball announcer attained network status until Bill White in the 1970s with CBS Radio and ABC-TV.

As the color line fell haltingly team by team, black players and the first wave of Latino players found themselves almost an island unto themselves.

Two minutes of audiotape of Robinson working in the ABC booth in Dodger Stadium with Leo Durocher and Chris Schenkel on September 6, 1965, were recorded off Moline, Illinois's WQAD-TV by brothers Steve and John Ring of Galesburg. That is the entire known surviving record of Robinson's broadcast work. A copy was sent to Rachel Robinson in New York in 2013.

But like his original role drawing attention to larger societal issues, Robinson seemed to be above the scratching, chewing life of a coach and the pontificating of a baseball announcer. He and his family participated in the 1963 civil rights March on Washington. His voice was always heard on social and political issues. Dr. Martin Luther King Jr. always gave him credit, claiming he would not have had his own profile in civil rights without Robinson paving the way.

Baseball provides so many metaphors for life. We're still filling out the rosters with newcomers previously unwelcome. Robinson would tell us we still have many proverbial innings to play. We've scored early. But we dare not stop now, or the teams of regression— always lurking—will catch us.

The No. 42, permanently retired throughout baseball, the only number given such an honor, is our ultimate reminder of the highest standard to uphold.

Babe Ruth

Modern Baseball's Narrative Follows in the Bambino's Wake

Exalted in his status as a baseball senior statesman and regal in his bearing, Joe DiMaggio nevertheless yielded to a higher power when queried about his all-time baseball ranking.

The Yankee Clipper was being pulled in all directions at the 1991 dedication of his statue at the National Italian-American Sports Hall of Fame. A producer needed him to appear before a TV camera, but Joltin' Joe shooed him off. He had made a commitment to talk to a small group of writers, and he was going to honor it.

Already ranked the "greatest living ballplayer," DiMaggio was startled when told that some even rated him with Babe Ruth. That was near-blasphemy.

NO. 1

"I'm really honored that people would compare me with the Babe," said DiMaggio, who then gazed skyward. "The Babe's up there." He did not just mean heaven. DiMaggio placed Ruth in a well-deserved position—above everyone else, including him, in baseball's pantheon. He had made his Yankees debut a year after Ruth had departed for the Boston Braves. Even then, Ruth had evolved into legend. Some had even tagged him with the ability to call his own World Series–busting shots.

Ruth was the ultimate game changer and thus achieves the top ranking of all persons, events, and innovations that have moved through baseball. Everything about the big lug was outsized—his talent as the American League's best lefty starter, then his dominance as its greatest-ever pure slugger. Add on Ruth's enormous appetites for food, sex, and fast cars, and he was a true colossus striding atop the entertainment world in his own time and beyond.

Ruth may have been sports' greatest-ever personality, evoking a standard by which much has been measured by the near-century since his prime. His nicknames "The Bambino" and "Sultan of Swat" are all-timers. Titanic homers by sluggers who followed him over the next

Babe Ruth's powerful swing led baseball from the
Dead Ball Era into the era of the home run.

80 years are "Ruth-ian clouts." His name is otherwise dropped in a thousand other ways. And why shouldn't it be? By himself, he totally transformed baseball—instantaneously—from the pitch-and-putt offensive game of the Dead Ball Era into a sport built around power. Lineups today are constructed in the same manner as Ruth's 1920s-vintage New York Yankees. The order features preferably a left-handed-hitting big bopper batting third, like Ruth, followed by several other strongmen. No devolution to the spray-the-ball-around style while pitchers try to stop the slash hitters with spitballs has ever gotten any traction.

Ruth's signature records became part of baseball's Ten Commandments. His 60 homers in a season and 714 career homers were considered almost set in stone. The initial attempts to conquer these marks—by Roger Maris for the season record in 1961 and Henry Aaron for the career mark in 1973-74—became controversial national stories that spilled over from the sports pages. Traditionalists so admired Ruth's records that they showered pressure and vituperation upon Maris and Aaron, making their quests ordeals rather than joyous journeys. Unfortunately, many of Aaron's critics combined their Ruth-upholding attitudes with racism.

Everything about the big lug was outsized—his talent as the American League's best lefty starter, then his dominance as its greatest-ever pure slugger. Add on Ruth's enormous appetites for food, sex, and fast cars.

In the process of transforming the game, Ruth established the Yankees as baseball's longest-lasting dynasty and top road gate attraction while enabling construction of the massive Yankee Stadium. The Bronx Bombers have only vacated their status as baseball's most prominent team for relatively short periods since Ruth teamed with Lou Gehrig to power the Yankees to frequent one-team rule over the American League.

Ruth had feet of clay. He was often uncouth. He ignored and serial-cheated on first wife Helen, by all accounts a good person. Yet overall he was an approachable, friendly personality who spread good cheer in his sports persona and posed for practically any photo requested, often in a variety of unusual situations and outfits. Hardly anyone in baseball could dislike him.

"You never met a nicer guy in your life than Babe Ruth," was a February 13, 1994, remembrance by 1938 Brooklyn Dodger Woody English, who played during Ruth's one-year first-base coaching stint at Ebbets Field. Prior to Brooklyn, English had been a close-up witness as Cubs third baseman to Ruth's alleged "called shot" in the 1932 World Series at Wrigley Field, yet always denied Ruth had pointed to the bleachers an instant before.

"Sometimes I was sorry that I even said he didn't point for that home run," English said. "I liked him. We all liked him."

Ruth first burst on the scene as the Red Sox's southpaw ace, winning 64 games between 1915 and 1917, leading the American League in ERA with 1.75 in 1916 and starting a scoreless streak in the World Series that eventually reached 29²/₃ innings. All the while, though, another talent began bubbling to the surface—Ruth's bat. He slugged nine homers in his prime pitching seasons while batting at least .315 twice. Very soon he was doing double duty—taking his rotation turn while logging time in the outfield and first base on his off-days from the mound. In 1918, Ruth led the AL with 11 homers while batting an even .300 in the war-abbreviated season.

When the schedule returned to normalcy in 1919, Ruth wanted to be a full-time position player. Boston manager Ed Barrow, with whom Ruth would clash in upcoming years as a Yankee, still craved his left arm. Ruth made 15 starts with a 9-5 record in 1919. But he turned baseball on its ear, establishing himself as its No. 1 gate attraction, with 29 homers that season, besting Ed Williamson's antediluvian 1884 home-run record by two.

In spite of Ruth's towering status as baseball's best player, cash-strapped and debt-laden Red Sox owner Harry Frazee concocted the ultimate bailout-plan by selling Ruth to the affluent Yankees after the 1919 campaign. The long-term after-effects for both teams somehow morphed into talk of a curse, as in *Boston Globe* columnist Dan Shaughnessy's 1990 *Curse of the Bambino* book. But like the Chicago Cubs' "billy goat curse," the only hex afoot was the curse of bad management—the incompetency of both Frazee and Cubs' owner Phil Wrigley.

Ruth was truly made for New York. He established his own new power standards with 54 homers in 1920—which would be like a player belting 90 today. George Sisler of the St. Louis Browns was AL runner-up in 1920 with just 19 homers. Ruth then lifted the bar even further with 59 in 1921 to establish what might be the best all-around run-production season in history. That season's line also included 177 runs, 204 hits, 44 doubles, 16 triples, 168 RBIs, 145 walks, a .378

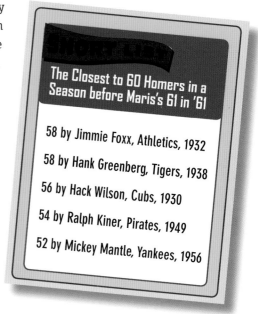

The Closest to 60 Homers in a Season before Maris's 61 in '61

58 by Jimmie Foxx, Athletics, 1932

58 by Hank Greenberg, Tigers, 1938

56 by Hack Wilson, Cubs, 1930

54 by Ralph Kiner, Pirates, 1949

52 by Mickey Mantle, Yankees, 1956

average, a .512 on-base percentage, an .846 slugging percentage, and a 1.359 OPS. Once again, his timing was exquisite. Commissioner Kenesaw Mountain Landis banned the eight Black Sox players for life late in the 1921 season. Baseball needed a positive story to counter-balance the ugliness of its worst-ever scandal. What it got was superhuman.

Amid conflicts with Landis, Barrow, and Yankees manager Miller Huggins, Ruth established himself as one of the top celebrities of the Roaring Twenties. He amassed three more 40-homer seasons through 1926 as other newbie sluggers failed to match his numbers. Finally he had his best-remembered season in 1927, when he set the record with 60 homers to lead a 110-44 Yankees team considered by many the best in baseball history. Only two players—the Athletics' Jimmie Foxx in 1932 and the Tigers' Hank Greenberg in 1938—would take serious runs at the season record with 58 each in their peak seasons, until Maris needed the newly expanded schedule and the 162nd game to reach 61 in '61.

Ruth teamed with Lou Gehrig and a supporting cast to provide the "five o'clock lightning" (the time of late innings during the afternoon-only games) that proved to be the bane of opponents. Interestingly, the massive production of the two great southpaw swingers did not always translate into pennants. With Foxx, the Athletics outlasted the Yankees to win three straight pennants from 1929 until 1931, until owner-manager Connie Mack had to trade off players to cut expenses as the Depression worsened.

Near the bottom of the crash on October 1, 1932, facts met legend for one of baseball's most seminal moments—of course involving Ruth. In Game 3 of the World Series at Wrigley Field, Ruth supposedly pointed to the bleachers before a strike-two pitch from Cubs ace Charlie Root. Seconds later, Ruth smashed a tape-measure homer to nearly that exact spot.

"It caused more excitement at that time than the Roosevelt-Hoover election," recalled English over the phone from his Newark, Ohio, home in 1994 during a *Diamond Gems* radio interview joined in the studio by Hall of Famer Billy Williams and former All-Star second baseman Glenn Beckert. English had teamed up with Cubs player-manager Charlie Grimm to give Democratic presidential candidate Franklin D. Roosevelt an autographed baseball at his box seat before the World Series game.

The super-charged atmosphere, also witnessed by a young John Paul Stevens, the future Supreme Court justice, was just as intriguing as the concept of Ruth calling his shot. New Yorkers had been agitated at the Cubs' decision to award ex-Yankees shortstop Mark Koenig, acquired down the stretch by Chicago, with just a half-share of World Series money. As Cubs captain, English had supervised the team vote on shares.

"We voted two-three times," English said. "We finally wound up with half a share. The Yankees picked it up and they really went bananas about Koenig. They called us cheap Chicago Cubs, tightwads, scrooges. I think we got a $4,000 share."

A huge crowd, most of them enthusiastic about the Yankees, greeted Ruth and wife Claire when they arrived at the Chicago train station in advance of Game 3. But one woman spit on Claire Ruth. Then, before Game 3, fans in Wrigley's left field bleachers threw lemons at Ruth, who soaked up the attention.

Then the Cubs' bench went to work on Ruth when he came to the plate in the fifth inning.

"We had quite a few bench jockeys on the team," English said. "Every player on the bench was yelling and called him every name under the book, most of them not complimentary. Ruth had two strikes. I'm facing him directly at third base. He's looking right in our dugout and he holds two fingers up. The pressbox was quite a ways back behind the stands and it looked like to them like he might have pointed. But he absolutely did not."

Few media accounts mentioned Ruth pointing. Later, though, as the called-shot tale began circulating, Ruth never denied pointing. Always a showman, he knew a good story.

Just before English's radio appearance in 1994, a home movie that had been stashed away for more than six decades surfaced, apparently showing Ruth pointing toward the Cubs dugout.

"I'll send him a Christmas card," English said of the film's owner.

English had been joined by fellow Cubs infielders Billy Jurges at shortstop and Billy Herman at second base, who in their senior years denied Ruth had called his shot. English ended up as the last living on-field witness, passing away at 91 in 1997.

Ruth was not finished hitting dramatic homers in Chicago. In the first All-Star Game the following summer at old Comiskey Park, he hit the thrilling, game-winning clout.

He never got the chance to manage his beloved Yankees, and just missed out on managerial opportunities with the Red Sox and Tigers.

From that point on, Ruth's career petered out. He slugged his final three homers on a memorable day in Pittsburgh's Forbes Field in 1935. He never got the chance to manage his beloved Yankees, and just missed out on managerial opportunities with the Red Sox and Tigers. Except for his one-year stint as a Dodgers coach, he never worked in baseball again before dying of cancer at 53 in 1948.

Despite the Maris and Aaron efforts, Ruth's feats stand the test of time. Barry Bonds (once), Mark McGwire (twice), and Sammy Sosa (three times) all hit more than 60 in a season, and Bonds surpassed Aaron's 755 career homers. But they were tainted by connections with PEDs. The Ruth/Aaron/Maris triumvirate has retained its legitimacy in the baseball world.

The Bambino stood out at several levels above everyone else, seemingly competing in a league better than the majors, at a stratospheric level far above the other mere mortals who played the game. Ruth changed baseball enough for two or three or a hundred men.

The American League

The Junior Circuit Roils Baseball to Create the Modern Game

NO. **6**

The National League had long been ripe for the picking. But providing competition for the fan dollar, if not the rooters' number one allegiance, required just the right timing and nerve.

Ban Johnson, assisted by Charles Comiskey, had both. And after the American League was born, the present competitive structure of baseball came into being.

Several attempts to compete with the established NL had been attempted in the last two decades of the 19th century. The eight-team American Association and the Northwestern League, comprised of smaller Midwest cities, set up shop in 1882-83. Players rebelling against the penurious salary structure set up the Players National League for the 1890 season.

Two years later, the NL had a monopoly on professional baseball. The Northwestern League had never achieved big-league status. The Players League lasted one year. And the American Association finally quit after 1891. The NL ballooned to 12 teams, taking on four American Association franchises in St. Louis, Baltimore, Washington, DC, and Louisville.

But as President Theodore Roosevelt tried to demonstrate in another decade, monopolies generally are not good. The NL actually suffered through the rest of the 1890s, thanks partially to a Depression-wracked economy and largely to its own failings. Baseball's sole major league was described by baseball historian Richard Lindberg in his *Stealing First in a Two-Team Town* memoir of the White Sox as a "weakened and politically corrupt National League, about to collapse under the weight of interlocking ownership, disgruntled players, and sagging attendance in financially troubled markets."

The American League club presidents of 1914: Frank Navin, Detroit; Benjamin S. Minor, Washington; Frank Farrell, New York; Charles Comiskey, Chicago; Ban Johnson, AL president; Joseph Lannin, Boston.

In 1894, a reorganized Western League, a minor league, appointed Cincinnati sportswriter Ban Johnson as president. The moves were backed by Chicago native Comiskey, a pioneering defensive player (the initial first baseman to play off the bag to stop ground balls), who soon acquired controlling interest in the league's St. Paul franchise.

Johnson revived the Western League, then rebranded the circuit as the American League for the 1900 season. He sought franchises in major eastern and midwestern cities to compete with the NL. Comiskey moved his St. Paul franchise to Chicago's South Side. And while Johnson was at first turned away when he sought an accommodation with the NL and status as a major league, his timing was perfect. The NL had contracted to eight teams, providing a talent pool of unemployed players. Johnson's teams actively recruited disgruntled NL players by abrogating the reserve system. In addition to Comiskey's White Stockings and franchises in Detroit, Cleveland, and Milwaukee, the AL fielded clubs in NL cities Philadelphia and Boston, and former NL cities Baltimore and Washington, DC. When Johnson succeeded in transferring the troubled Baltimore franchise to New York, where it set up shop in 1903 as the Highlanders—10 years before acquiring the game's royal name, Yankees—he had the leverage for peace with the NL.

The peace parlay immediately set up a World Series between the leagues. The Fall Classic has been held ever since except for 1904, when angry management withheld the New York Giants from the event, and 1994, canceled by acting commissioner Bud Selig due to the catastrophic players' strike. Almost immediately, the AL provided a much-needed spur to baseball interest. Total big-league attendance in 1903 was 4.7 million, compared to just 1.7 million for the sputtering NL in 1900.

The "hitless wonder" White Sox upset the record-breaking 116-victory Cubs in the 1906 World Series. Connie Mack's Philadelphia Athletics won the Fall Classic in 1910, 1911, and 1913. Led by Ty Cobb and Tris Speaker, many of the game's best players thrived as lifelong American Leaguers. A young lefty starter named Babe Ruth lifted the Boston Red Sox to short-term dominance starting in 1915. And a skilled lefty hitter named "Shoeless Joe" Jackson, acquired from Cleveland in 1915, led a White Sox powerhouse as World War I got underway.

In 1920, two concurrent events altered the AL's history. Ruth had been traded to the Yankees by the financially strained Red Sox, finding his destiny as the game's greatest slugger and personality. The Yankees went on to dominate the AL as a dynasty with few down periods all the way through 1964. Meanwhile, Jackson was enmeshed in the Black Sox Scandal in 1920 as the most serious gambling event of a game beset by attempted fixes for decades. The resulting banning of Jackson and seven of his teammates flushed serious gambling out of the system, but also weakened the White Sox franchise so drastically that, to this day, it remains locked in second-team status in Chicago.

Although the AL continued to host Hall of Famers like Lou Gehrig, Joe DiMaggio, Ted Williams, and Bob Feller, it eventually fell behind the NL in competitive quality by the 1950s due to both the Yankees' hegemony and slow movement toward integration. AL owners were comparatively more conservative than their NL counterparts in signing African-American players a decade after Jackie Robinson broke in with the Brooklyn Dodgers. Players of color began dominating the NL with MVP seasons in the 1950s, while the Detroit Tigers and Boston Red Sox were the last two big-league franchises to integrate in 1958 and 1959, respectively. The Yankees brought Elston Howard to the big-league roster in 1955. Harry "Suitcase" Simpson, the Yankees' second black player, arrived as a platoon performer in 1957. But the Bombers did not acquire a second

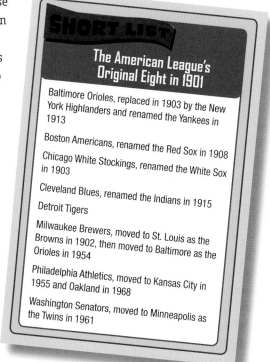

SHORT LIST

The American League's Original Eight in 1901

Baltimore Orioles, replaced in 1903 by the New York Highlanders and renamed the Yankees in 1913

Boston Americans, renamed the Red Sox in 1908

Chicago White Stockings, renamed the White Sox in 1903

Cleveland Blues, renamed the Indians in 1915

Detroit Tigers

Milwaukee Brewers, moved to St. Louis as the Browns in 1902, then moved to Baltimore as the Orioles in 1954

Philadelphia Athletics, moved to Kansas City in 1955 and Oakland in 1968

Washington Senators, moved to Minneapolis as the Twins in 1961

significant player of color until Panamanian Hector Lopez arrived in 1959, and no additional mainstay African American until Al Downing joined the starting rotation in 1963.

The talent imbalance due to the dominance of NL African Americans continued into the 1970s, when the institution of the designated hitter provided a happy home for older or defensively challenged hitters and transformed the AL into a more offensively oriented league. Adding to an old reputation as a "breaking-ball league" for its pitchers, a separate style of baseball developed in the AL with pitchers not batting and managers not forced to yank their starters for pinch hitters or make late-inning double switches.

The distinction between the leagues has long been blurred due to the abolition of the league presidencies, the combining of umpiring staffs, and interleague play. And yet shreds of the old AL's original identity remain, the upstart that rose to dominance.

Four Balls, Three Strikes

The Basic Rules and Variations Set Up Baseball's Strategy

No one alive can remember a game without "working the count," "painting the corners" or any of the other necessary strategies tilting the balance of the pitcher against the hitter. The game's competitive flow centers on skillful manipulation of the ball-and-strike count.

But early- and mid-19th century forms of "base ball" involved the pitcher as a mere "feeder" of the ball so a batsman could strike it cleanly to evade the glove-less fielders. However, early pitchers with their underhanded deliveries did try to throw off the hitters with intentionally bad serves to make them lunge and take the oomph out of their hits. Countering such tactics, batters began taking pitches. Opposite to over-aggressive, first-ball-swinging hitters of the 21st century, some batters allowed dozens of pitches to go by before they swung, infuriating all involved in the game with the plodding pace. Think of it as an ancient precursor of the meandering pace of modern games with three innings eating up more than two hours.

To counter this maddening trend, early rules makers instituted the first formal system of called balls and strikes in 1864. But the system was only a start. The count only was triggered when the umpire decided either the pitcher or batter was stalling. While aimed at restoring balance between hurler and batsman, the new system actually allowed the home-plate umpire to assume his everlasting role of primacy as the third party in the ball-and-strike duels. The umpire now had the responsibility of determining batters' and pitchers' intentions.

In 1875, the umpire was mandated to call a ball on "each third unfair ball delivered." When three balls total were called, the batter was awarded first base. In 1881, the rule was further modified for the umpire to call every pitch a ball or strike.

This 1895 Calvert Lithographing Co. "base ball" poster inspires little confidence that the umpire will call a good game.

The maximum number of balls and strikes remained somewhat fluid during the transformative 1880s, when many facets of baseball began to resemble today's game. Finally, in 1889, four balls and three strikes became the standard.

Accompanying fine-tuning of the rules involved foul balls. Part of the batter's stalling tactics against the pitcher in the mid-19th century involved deliberately fouling pitches, which did not count as strikes. Only one advantage accrued to the defense with this tactic—batters were ruled out if the foul was caught on one bounce. The counting of fouls as strikes on less than a two-strike count came relatively late in baseball's development—in 1901 in the National League and 1903 in the newly founded American League. While the 19th century featured platoons of skilled bat-handlers who could intentionally foul pitches for long stretches, the talent did not totally die out as the 20th century reached its maturity. The likes of Luke "Old Aches and Pains" Appling and select other bat-handlers could rack up impressive foul-ball totals on two strikes, adding to the burdens of pitchers who were virtually mandated to go nine innings at the time.

The final part of the equation of balls and strikes came with the conception of a formal strike zone. Early baseball, oriented toward the hitter, required the pitcher to deliver his serve to the batter's liking, such as waist-high. Yet the earliest criticism of umpires came when they had varied interpretations of how close those pitches came to the batter's desired spot. The initial visual conception of a strike zone came in 1871 as rules were changed to require the batter to call for either a "high" or "low" pitch. The zone for the former ranged between the shoulder and the waist, and for the latter between the waist and the knee. Put together they formed the basic strike zone going forward.

Early baseball, oriented toward the hitter, required the pitcher to deliver his serve to the batter's liking, such as waist-high.

The lords of the game have adjusted the strike zone at modest lengths vertically at the knees and shoulders several times, depending on whether they wanted to dampen down or turn loose run production. Most recent was the expansion of the zone vertically in 1963, then contraction after 1968's "Year of the Pitcher." All along, pitchers, batters, and managers have waged countless battles—incurring ejections—with umpires over their interpretation of what really is a subjective visualization of the rules, varying slightly between each umpire simply because they are human.

How each end of the pitcher-batter confrontation worked four balls, three strikes governed their success. Pitchers with blazing fastballs were not afraid to leave their pitches up in the imaginary zone, trying to overpower hitters. Those with less speed tried to keep the balls down, sometimes borderline balls, so hitters could not square them. The result: infield groundballs.

On the Rare Three-Ball Walk

"Was that a three-ball walk? I only had three balls on my . . . Did you have four balls?" —*Nationals radio broadcaster Dave Jageler to partner Charlie Slowes when the Reds' Joey Votto was mistakenly given a walk after only three balls on May 31, 2015*

SPITBALLING

The pattern of "pitchers' pitches" and "hitters' pitches" became established. A pitcher getting ahead two strikes, no balls was considered to have the advantage. More often than not he'd "waste" a ball before working to put the hitter away. But if he fell behind, say 1-0 or 2-1, the advantage shifted to the hitter. Since fastballs were the pitch that typically were kept under the most control, the odds stated the batter could expect a fastball if the pitcher was behind. Exceptions were pitchers who had mastered a splitter or knuckleball.

The greatest control pitchers of different eras were perceived to get slightly wider strike zones, simply because they could work on the inside and outside corners and in a subtle manner keep expanding the zone, with the umpires' eyes following suit.

The combination of Hall of Famers Greg Maddux and Tom Glavine on the 1990s Atlanta Braves was a one-two punch of psychological warfare against hitters. Maddux's 20 walks (6 intentional) in 232 $^2/_3$ innings in 1997 was simply stupendous. However, the man whose tenacity and baseball-pacing intelligence earned him the nicknames "Mad Dog" and "The Professor" had occasions to adeptly use the strike zone that was concocted more than a century earlier. On one occasion Maddux said walking a particular hitter was not sin, but in fact strategically sound, given the circumstances.

In response, a strategy spreading through baseball as the new millennium got under way was to train hitters to work the counts and look over as many pitches as possible. A Red Sox-Yankees night game starting at 8:00 p.m. in the Eastern Time Zone for TV's sake meant a lot of bleary eyes due to the deliberate hitters on both sides.

The Farm System

Branch Rickey's Version of *Green Acres* Was No Sitcom

NO. **8**

No matter what his motivation, no matter how much Branch Rickey saw profit or savings from his decisions, his two greatest innovations bred long-term winning.

And baseball's bottom line on the financial ledger always is tied to the won-lost column tilting toward the left.

The calculated recruitment and development of Jackie Robinson to bust the color line had completed a spectacular Rickey twin killing that changed baseball for all time. Combining baseball savvy and nickel-biting acumen, Rickey already had pioneered the farm system that altered the way baseball procured and groomed talent. By the time Robinson broke in and became baseball's best all-around player as National League MVP in 1949, Rickey had developed a pair of development machines in the Cardinals and Dodgers.

With some lulls, those two organizations have been known for strong farm systems ever since. Even with the tools of free agency and international scouting—and with the bountiful talent pool in Cuba waiting to be tapped in full—strong farm systems are necessities for successful franchises. Those who financially skimp or mismanage player development end up going without a World Series championship for as long as 108 years.

The tried-and-true method of acquiring talent in the early 20th century was purchasing the best-producing players from the slew of independent minor-league clubs operating nationwide. Selling their best players to the majors became a necessary revenue stream for the minor-league operators. But with St. Louis ownerships that were never particularly well

Branch Rickey (right) hobnobbed with fellow big names—
such as Rogers Hornsby (center) and team owner Sam
Breadon (left)—during his tenure as Cardinals president.

heeled in the pre–Anheuser Busch decades, the Cardinals could not match teams from bigger cities dollar for dollar.

By the 1920s, concentrating on front-office work after long stints as a manager, the intellectual Rickey could put his theories into practice.

"Other clubs could outbid. They had money," Rickey recalled in a *Sporting News* interview. "I do not feel that the farming system we have established is the result of any inventive genius—it is the result of stark necessity. We did it to meet a question of supply and demand of young ballplayers."

Buying farm clubs and then stocking them with players—albeit ones signed cheaply—kept control of the development process. That would give Rickey a chance to separate the talent he wanted to keep with ones he would trade to fill other holes. All the while, he instituted newfangled methods of teaching.

The tried-and-true method of acquiring talent in the early 20th century was purchasing the best-producing players from the slew of independent minor-league clubs operating nationwide.

The strategy worked. Rickey developed two sets of consistent winners in St. Louis—a team that won a string of four pennants and two World Series between 1928 and 1934, and another near-dynasty that dominated the National League, winning four of the five pennants and two World Series between 1942 and 1946. The Dean brothers—Dizzy and Paul—along with Pepper Martin and Joe Medwick were homegrown leaders of the first batch of winners. Stan Musial and Enos Slaughter were the bulwarks of the final group.

As he did with Robinson, Rickey had to deal with resistance to his farm teams. Commissioner Kenesaw Mountain Landis disdained Rickey's system with a hidebound belief in independent, thriving minor leaguers not dependent on big-league baseball for their survival. The autocratic Landis twice released more than 70 of Rickey's farmhands, believing they had been stuck in the minors without chance of advancement.

But Rickey outlasted Landis. Moving over to the Dodgers in 1942, he re-created the Cardinals' development success with Brooklyn. Almost immediately, his scouts signed teenagers like Gil Hodges and Duke Snider. Although the signees were quick fodder for military service during World War II, Rickey knew he would gain their services (maturity added) after the war ended. At one point, the Dodgers had more than 700 players under contract. With near-military precision, they were trained via a system of colors and numbers at the new Vero Beach complex in Florida. With an influx of African Americans joining them starting in the 1940s, the Dodgers would rarely be out of a pennant race through 1966.

Rickey did not quite repeat his farm success nor achieve Dodgers-like integration with the Pirates, the last of three teams he ran from 1951 to 1955. The team never emerged out of sad-sack status during his watch. However, his legacy was Roberto Clemente, whom he helped steal out of the Dodgers system after the 1954 season, along with signing and developing eventual key contributors to the Buccos' 1960 World Series titlists like Bill Mazeroski, Dick Groat, Dick Stuart, and Bob Skinner.

Other franchises were able to mimic Rickey's systems over the ensuing decades. The hyping of farm systems became intensified with the emergence of *Baseball America* in the final two decades of the 20th century. In the end, ranking farm systems wasn't as important as the end result—when the prospects became big-league producers. Top-rated systems did not automatically translate into championships within the next decade.

SHORT LIST

Wacky Minor-League Team Names

Las Vegas 51s
Albuquerque Isotopes
Omaha Storm Chasers
Joliet Slammers
Lehigh Valley Iron Pigs
Hartford Yard Goats
Toledo Mud Hens
Lansing Lugnuts
El Paso Chihuahuas
Biloxi Shuckers
Wisconsin Timber Rattlers

Rickey would be proud of his Cardinals of the 2010s, still largely replenishing the talent base from within on yet another string of World Series contenders. The Twins have long possessed a productive development program, but the full effects have been lost due to finances. The core of the 1987 and 1991 Twins World Series winners were homegrown, yet the periods before and after have been barren of titles. First penurious owner Calvin Griffith, then the Pohlad family have been unable to retain most of the crown jewels of their system once they reached star-compensation status.

Another long-productive system that finally ran dry in 2014-15 was the Atlanta Braves. Known for homegrown pitching along with seeking players of good character, the Braves' record in developing run producers may have been unmatched in the game. A long string of hitters who either achieved, or came close, to the vaunted 30-homer, 100-RBI level either in Atlanta or elsewhere spewed forth starting with Ron Gant in 1987.

Rickey never came up with the slogan, "See Tomorrow's Stars Today." But the concept was clear. And baseball is better for his innovation based on necessity.

Minnie Minoso
The Jackie Robinson of Latino Baseball Players

Minnie Minoso sat off to the far left, better to let the men who had followed him take center stage. In the conference center of U.S. Cellular Field in the spring of 2014, he was joined by catcher Adrian Nieto, outfielder Dayan Viciedo, shortstop Alexei Ramirez, and first baseman Jose Abreu. It was a panel of proud Cubans.

The scene recalled baseball's past, when Cuba was the centerpiece of the modest number of Latino players filtering into the majors. And now there was an apparent thaw of ancient Cold War relations between Cuba and the United States. Perhaps the talent collection also suggested a robust future for Cuban ballplayers in Major League Baseball.

Past is almost always prologue in baseball. History hung heavy in this gathering to highlight the White Sox's Cuban Connection. The joyful Minoso, by all estimates at least 88 at this gathering, was the patron saint of all the others in the room. He represented the breaking of a second kind of baseball color line—a black Latino who could enter the majors, thrive, and keep his joyful personality amid the prejudice and cultural chasms of the 1950s. This man paved the road for so many Latinos, including Hall of Famer Roberto Clemente.

The Hall of Fame was brought up once again to Minoso, who surely would have qualified if his employment address in the 1950s had been Yankee Stadium and not Comiskey Park, where the White Sox were perennial runners-up to the Bronx Bombers, whose players could take advantage of the world's media capital. Minoso crossed himself when Cooperstown was mentioned. His prayers were never answered in his lifetime, as he died suddenly in early 2015.

Baseball could not function now without its full complement of Latino players, now pushing the 30 percent mark in the game. But prior to Minoso's cup of coffee with the Indians in 1949 and trade to the White Sox in 1951, which established him as one of the

NO. 9

Minnie Minoso—"The Cuban Comet"—with the early-1950s White Sox in effect knocked down an informal color line for all Spanish-speaking players to come.

game's most exciting players, any players from the Caribbean or Mexico had to be light-skinned. Two Cubans on the Reds in the early 20th century were described in the press as "pure as a bar of Castilian soap," meaning they were of Spanish aristocratic heritage with no drop of African blood. Dark-skinned Latinos crept into the game one by one after Minoso. There was no signing surge as with the integration of rosters with African Americans. Sandy Amoros was a part-time left fielder for the Brooklyn Dodgers, distinguishing himself with a circus catch in the 1955 World Series. Meanwhile, 20-year-old black Puerto Rican Clemente had just completed his rookie season with the Pirates, who nabbed him for $4,000 in the November 1954 draft from Brooklyn's Triple-A Montreal roster. Crack Pirates scout Howie Haak wasn't fooled by the Dodgers' attempt to hide Clemente, and he notified boss Branch Rickey, with whom he had once worked in Brooklyn.

Impressed by Clemente's five-tool talents, Rickey dispatched Haak to tour Latin America to find more of his kind. Haak would go on to become baseball's pre-eminent scout south of the border with the Pirates employing the most Latinos of any team by the late 1960s. The roster's Latino complement enabled manager Danny Murtaugh to field the majors' first all–black and Latino lineup on September 1, 1971. "We thank God for him. He opened the door for us," said Pirates catcher Manny Sanguillen, a Panamanian, upon Haak's death in 1999.

On the heels of his 2014 AL Rookie of the Year Award, Cuban product Jose Abreu of the White Sox, pictured here helping autistic youths enjoy baseball

Haak recruited the talent, then the regal Clemente led them on the field and in the clubhouse. The Great One was one of baseball's most respected players, distinguishing himself in the 1971 World Series, and amassing 3,000 hits before his tragic death in a plane crash on an earthquake-relief mission to Nicaragua on New Year's Eve 1972. Earning respect was a hard-won process for Clemente, fellow Hall of Famer Orlando Cepeda, and many star Latinos trying to fit in to a new culture, learn a new language, and deal with overt racism.

Cepeda was a Puerto Rican whose Giants actually leaped into the forefront of Latino signings by augmenting his slugging presence at the dawn of the 1960s with four great Dominican signees— Hall of Famer Juan Marichal and the three outfield-playing Alou brothers—Felipe, Matty, and Jesus. But the Latino numbers were nowhere near those of 21st-century baseball.

Misunderstanding was spread by sportswriters. Les Biederman of the *Pittsburgh Press* quoted Clemente phonetically with his struggling English, rather than cleaning up the grammar, when he first came up: "I no play so gut yet. Me like hot weather, veree hot. I no run fast cold weather. No get warm in cold. No get warm, no play gut." Some managers were intolerant of the cultural difference. Chuck Dressen of the Senators ordered his four Cubans to learn English quickly. Cuban Luis Tiant said Indians manager Joe Adcock threatened to fine his Latin players $200 if they spoke Spanish around the clubhouse or dugout. Alvin Dark, centerpiece of some racial tension on the early 1960s Giants, forbade his Latin players to converse in Spanish on the team bus.

Alvin Dark, centerpiece of some racial tension on the early 1960s Giants, forbade his Latin players to converse in Spanish on the team bus.

But prejudice within the game finally began to abate. So the Pirates' competitors, along with key American League teams, began to boost their Latin scouting efforts in the 1970s.

Dallas Green, 1980 World Series champion manager of the Phillies and former Phillies farm director, recalled, "Ruben Amaro Sr. had all the contacts in Venezuela and the Dominican and Mexico. We were one of the first groups to tie into relationships. We carried it into Chicago. He signed some great kids at 15, 16, got them started in pro careers. Juan Samuel, George Bell, Julio Franco."

Blue Jays GM Pat Gillick was right on the Phillies' heels, and soon "was instrumental in getting a leg up" on many teams, said Green. By the 1980s, Toronto, now a contender, became a leader in Latin signings. More recently, the Texas Rangers have come to the forefront as almost every organization operates sophisticated baseball academies in the Dominican and Venezuela.

The actual length and breadth of Latin scouting has expanded further south beyond Venezuela. Three players out of Brazil have been signed. But Cuba remains the last fruitful market waiting to be fully tapped in the Western Hemisphere.

"You're going to see a greater influence now with Cuba opening up," said Gordon Lakey, pro scouting director of the Phillies. "The players are getting out a lot easier than they used to. Early on, when you got the first new Cuban players, basically it was an emphasis on pitchers like El Duque. Now there's such a dearth of offensive players, so they'll be looking for hitters."

He who hesitates to sign the heirs to Minnie Minoso's legacy is truly lost in baseball.

SPRAGUE, P. Chicago

Pitching Overhand from 60 Feet, 6 Inches

The Decisions That Ensured Baseball Would Not Become Softball

The act of propelling a baseball, the elbow exhibiting maximum torque, at 102 mph plateward from the leverage of a mound might have been an absolute flight of fancy in baseball of the mid-19th century.

The pitcher was indeed just that—a relatively secondary figure charged with delivering the baseball to a spot of the batsman's liking. From there, it was a battle of wits and skills between the hitter and fielders attempting to retire the man, now touring the bases. No baseball figure of the game's first era could envision the pitcher, using a delivery that strains the outer limits of muscle and sinew, becoming the dominant factor in the game.

Baseball changes at a glacial pace, but changes nevertheless. Thus was the case with the concept of pitching, its deliveries and location and leverage against the hitter. The end result—more than a century after the Civil War—was pitching so dominant that baseball had to change its physical properties—lowering the mound—to boost offense after 1968, "Year of the Pitcher," and Bob Gibson's 1.12 ERA. Almost every ensuing tweak has been undertaken to ease the hitters' task in sports' most difficult skill set.

An Old Judge Cigarettes baseball card featuring an underhand delivery by Charlie Sprague of the Chicago White Stockings

The original pitching concept featured a natural throwing motion. An underarm delivery is so much more kinetic for body chemistry than the massively stressful overhand motion. Most forms of softball employ an underarm motion no matter what the speed of the delivery. But the professional nature of baseball after 1869 prompted pitchers to seek every edge possible, and thus baseball became more than just softball played with a regulation hardball.

The earliest pitchers could not overpower the batters anyway. The pace-setting New York Knickerbockers, who defined early baseball rules, established pitching distance at 15 paces or 45 feet in 1854. The pitcher was, for want of a better word, a moving tee. The ball could not be "jerked." It was pitched, not thrown, as in pitching a horseshoe. Balls were pitched in a stiff-armed, stiff-wristed manner that had evolved from cricket, one of baseball's ancestral games. The arm had to pass below the hip as the ball was delivered.

But as baseball evolved into a play-for-pay system, pitchers began experimenting, first with a change of pace, then with curveballs. Naturally, new deliveries were required. The pressure on rules-makers mounted. By 1872 bent-elbow and jerked deliveries were allowed. Pitchers could deliver the ball from a waist-high release, and the hurlers were pushing farther upward. By the 1880s the familiar overhand delivery became the preferred method of pitchers.

With this rapid evolution, the 45-foot distance gave way. By 1881, the pitching line was moved back to 50 feet. But even at this distance the pitchers were increasingly overpowering the hitters. Remaining restrictions against deliveries were eliminated for the 1885 season. More strikeout sprees ensued.

Finally, for the 1893 season, the National League voted to move the distance back to the standard 60 feet, 6 inches. The pitchers' front delivery line was actually moved back just

On Cy Young's 1891 Delivery

"He winds up his arm, then his body, then his legs, bows profoundly to his great outfield, straightens up again, then lets her go. It is difficult to tell whether the ball comes from his hands or his feet." —*Peter Morris,* A Game of Inches

SPITBALLING

another five feet, to 55 feet. But a slab from which the pitcher's back leg would start replaced the back of the five-and-a-half-foot pitchers' box, so the present distance was established.

Speed and leverage were augmented by the deception of often elaborate windups.

Hall of Famer Cy Young modified his delivery, to spectacular effect: He used a quintet of 30-plus-victory seasons to amass a record 511 victories. Windups where the pitchers' arms met over their heads remained a staple of deliveries well into the last third of the 20th century. Eventually, the scientific study of pitching, corresponding with pitch counts and the beginning of the five-man rotation, led to more simplified pre-release motion. Too much money was at stake with unnecessary movement and awkward mechanics. Don Larsen's World Series perfect game in 1956, accomplished without windup, was a role model.

The quest for sheer speed was part of pitching's refinement. The ability to determine whether farmboy fireballer Bob Feller actually threw 100 mph was inaccurate in pre–radar gun days, so gimmicks like having Feller throw while a speeding police motorcycle tried to match his pitch pace were undertaken. Baltimore Orioles' lefty phenom Steve Dalkowski was estimated to throw in the low 100 mph range in the early 1960s, but his abject wildness did not allow him to rise above Triple-A as he amassed a 46-80 minor-league record.

The ability to determine whether farmboy fireballer Bob Feller actually threw 100 mph was inaccurate in pre–radar gun days, so gimmicks like having Feller throw while a speeding police motorcycle tried to match his pitch pace were undertaken.

Finally, a somewhat cumbersome radar device was tried on Nolan Ryan in Anaheim in 1974. He was measured at 100. Now, the portable guns show Reds closer Aroldis Chapman commonly tickling 102 mph in the ninth inning. These century-speed-busters should consider themselves fortunate that 19th-century rules makers mandated the short 60 feet, 6 inches as the standard rubber-to-plate distance. When 6'10" Hall of Famer Randy Johnson was in his prime, he combined speed with maximum leverage, and many hitters had the illusion of The Big Unit almost reaching out and touching them on his way to 4,875 career strikeouts.

Somewhere, the ghost of a Knickerbocker cackles. You ever hear of those underhanding pitchers having Tommy John surgery? The local park-district softball chucker, complete with beer belly, pitches well into his 40s or even 50s. Even with modern sports medicine and critically analyzed pitching mechanics, the long line of injured pitchers still marches into the orthopedic surgeons' offices. The harder they throw, the more likely they seem to break down. In the end, throwing overhand for both speed and deception is like cutting a deal with the devil. El Diablo inevitably asks for the arm back.

Fielding Gloves

Gold Gloves Mined from Catchers' Sore Hands

NO. **11**

What would baseball be without gloves at all nine defensive positions? Maybe a variation of softball?

Actually, most forms of softball also use gloves in the field. The only recognizable off-shoot that exposes bare hands to the inevitable fractures and dislocations is the slow-pitch 16-inch softball game played in the Chicago area.

Gloves became a necessity in baseball's early professional days in the 1880s as pitching began to evolve into an overhand delivery with more speed. Catchers, originally standing farther behind the batter than where they crouch today, could not continue to handle the faster serves without constant injury to their hands. In turn, as the game further picked up its pace and sophistication, first basemen needed gloves to scoop low throws from the other infielders. Not long before the 19th century turned, every defensive player wore a primitive version of today's flexible, encompassing gloves.

The obvious need for any kind of cushion for the hands in fielding the baseball was apparent from the game's antediluvian roots. But the early-macho codes of baseball frowned upon such aids. "Fear of ridicule for violating the ideal of manliness," wrote Peter Morris in his historical narrative *A Game of Inches*. "While many early players must have considered wearing gloves, they were deterred by the possibility of being stigmatized."

Morris speculated the first player to wear a glove, basically similar to a workman's glove, was catcher Ben Delavergne of the amateur Knickerbockers club of Albany, New York, around 1860. Pioneering pro catcher Deacon White, finally inducted into the Hall of Fame in 2013,

Bill Mazeroski won eight Gold Gloves at second base for the Pirates.

reportedly wore a large buckskin glove in 1872. The next step was the invention of the catcher's mitt. Morris described how catcher Joe Gunson of Kansas City stitched together the fingers of his glove, and added padding, to cobble together a first-generation tool of ignorance in 1888.

Within a decade, almost all pro players wore gloves in the field. Still, gloves remained small enough to basically fit the contours of a player's hand. The throwing hand was needed to help snare baseballs as one-handed catches were done at the player's peril. The fielder needed to catch the baseball squarely in the glove's pocket to ensure the play. But the gloves vastly improved with the introduction of the flexible heel, called the Edge-U-Cated Heel, in 1959. Catcher, shortstop, second base, and center field became positions known for defensive prowess. Later, first base, supposedly a repository for slow-footed, ham-handed sluggers, also was known for slick fielders like Keith Hernandez and Mark Grace. Bumble and fumble at first base, and you had a great baseball nickname, like Dick Stuart's "Dr. Strangeglove" and "Stonefinger."

At their own risk, managers and executives placed players with "iron gloves," mediocre range, or limited experience in the middle infield or center field to boost hitting. Sometimes they got away with it. In the 1968 World Series, Mayo Smith won it all after shifting center fielder Mickey Stanley to shortstop, replacing good-field, no-hit (.135) Ray Oyler. That move opened a regular outfield spot for Tigers legend Al Kaline, playing in his only Fall Classic.

Eventually, several notables from the 1950s onward became renowned for their fielding, earning Hall of Fame status.

Ozzie "The Wizard of Oz" Smith at shortstop and Bill Mazeroski at second booked their Cooperstown journeys primarily with their gloves, with Mazeroski (in 2001) the last player, other than the posthumously inducted Ron Santo in 2010, to be voted in by the various incarnations of the Hall's Veterans Committee. Luis Aparicio preceded Smith as a speedy gloveman at shortstop from 1956 to 1973. A case can also be made that Brooks Robinson's virtuoso performance at third base, befitting his "Human Vacuum Cleaner" tag, on the national stage in the 1970 World Series sealed an already-legitimate Cooperstown deal.

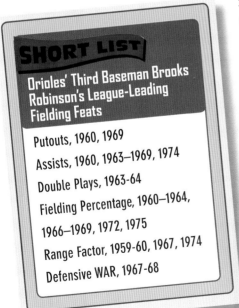

SHORT LIST

Orioles' Third Baseman Brooks Robinson's League-Leading Fielding Feats

Putouts, 1960, 1969

Assists, 1960, 1963–1969, 1974

Double Plays, 1963-64

Fielding Percentage, 1960–1964, 1966–1969, 1972, 1975

Range Factor, 1959-60, 1967, 1974

Defensive WAR, 1967-68

"You're talking about 6 inches or a foot, you wouldn't be making those plays," Robinson recalled. "You started to believe something special was happening in that series. I knew they were going to hit the ball my way. Being in four World Series and being the MVP [in the '70 Series] helped me get in the Hall of Fame."

Rawlings, one of the most prominent manufacturers of gloves, began the Gold Glove Award for each major-league defensive position in 1957, three years after players stopped leaving their gloves at their defensive positions during their turns to hit. In 1958, the Gold Glove was expanded to include two rosters—the top defensive producers from the American League and the National League.

Rawlings, one of the most prominent manufacturers of gloves, began the Gold Glove Award for each major-league defensive position in 1957.

Robinson, Smith, and Mazeroski thoroughly dominated the genre. Robinson won 16 straight Gold Gloves, all for the Orioles, between 1960 and 1975. Smith snared 13 in a row, divided between the Padres and Cardinals, between 1980 and 1992. Aparicio nailed nine in his 1956 to 1973 career, the number matching his AL-leading stolen-base total. "Maz" copped eight Gold Gloves from 1956 to 1972. Smith and Aparicio were .262 lifetime hitters, while Mazeroski finished at .260. Robinson batted .267 lifetime, but had 2,848 hits, of which 268 were homers. He was American League Most Valuable Player in 1964.

Interestingly, many fans and reporters consider the Gold Glove to be a popularity contest. Some pundits even theorized the award winner needed to amass good-to-great offensive numbers to even be considered. A .225 hitter would never cut it. Startling long balls are the singularly seminal moments for which Mazeroski and Smith were known. "Maz," of course, won the 1960 World Series with his Game 7 walk-off homer in Pittsburgh. Banjo-hitter Smith's game-winning homer against the Dodgers in Game 5 of the 1985 National League Championship Series in St. Louis gets frequent replay with the astonished play-by-play call of Jack Buck.

The runs they stopped count for even more. Acrobatic athleticism marked the best of Smith, Robinson, and Willie Mays with his "optical illusion" catch on Vic Wertz running straight back in center in the 1954 World Series.

But just making the routine plays at their positions wouldn't have been possible without their well-oiled gloves, developed and perfected over the decades. They are accoutrements the game could not have done without.

Free Agency

Peter Seitz's Emancipation Proclamation Benefited Labor and Management

The most outstanding example of baseball as an American outlaw organization was its "reserve clause."

Sports—led by baseball—was the only industry where mainstay workers could not choose to switch to another job when they were dissatisfied or when their contracts expired. A combination of essentially pro-monopoly court rulings, management arrogance, player ignorance, and lack of a savvy Marvin Miller–style labor advocate prior to 1966 kept players bound to their teams, theoretically into perpetuity.

The road to free agency was blocked until Players Association godfather Miller took over in 1966. He began a decade-long process that could not have been sped up no matter what legal tack he undertook. But Miller's gradualism, waiting for a key case that would establish precedent, worked like a dream for the pocketbooks of all. The end result was free agency, a now-established part of pro sports that has financially and artistically benefited both labor and management.

The term "reserve" in the clause that supposedly bound an athlete to his team for his career—unless traded or released—originated in 1879. The eight National League teams of that time would "reserve" five players, off-limits to any other team. Conveniently, the affected players were not at first informed of their indentured status. By 1883, a "Tripartite Agreement" among the three pro leagues of the day—the NL, the American Association, and Northwestern League—expanded the reserve list to 11 per team while also respecting each other's contracts to prevent players from jumping leagues. The players were further throttled when the owners imposed a $2,500 annual individual salary cap with pay tiers.

Andy Messersmith, newly freed by arbitrator Peter Seitz, tries out his new Atlanta Braves uniform.

The system became ingrained, never seriously challenged in a sport that trailed most other businesses in labor practices and worker rights. Successive court rulings granted baseball an anti-trust exemption, allowing owners to continue the reserve clause. If a player wanted to shop around his services at the highest level of the game, he had nowhere else to go. All along, the lords of baseball had operated illegally, but no advocate, arbitrator, or court called them on the violation. When Miller brought his steelworkers' union experience to the Players Association, he almost immediately red-flagged Paragraph 10-A of the uniform players contract. "The club shall have the right to renew this contract for the period of one year on the same terms," was the telling wording. That meant contracts in actuality had an end game, not automatic renewal at the team's pleasure, as was age-old practice.

Walter O'Malley, whose team wound up producing the free agent identified most closely with breaking baseball's reserve clause

After Miller had worked in the concept of arbitration to settle salary and other disputes into his bargaining agreements in the early 1970s, he had his perfect test cases. Pitcher Andy Messersmith declined to sign a new contract with the Los Angeles Dodgers in 1975 when owner Walter O'Malley, a line-in-the-sand man for management control of players, refused to grant him a no-trade clause. Miller filed to arbitrate the dispute. Similarly, lefty Dave McNally refused to sign a new contract after being traded from the Orioles to the Montreal Expos for the '75 season. McNally quit the Expos on June 8 due to a sore wrist, but allowed Miller to have him available in his legal bullpen as a backup case.

Baseball-appointed arbitrator Peter Seitz heard the case and decided in favor of the players. But his first preference was for both sides to settle the reserve-clause issue via collective bargaining.

"I begged them to negotiate," Seitz said. "The owners were too stupid and stubborn. They were like the French barons in the 12th century. They had accumulated so much power they couldn't share it with anybody."

Messersmith got a multi-year, $1.7 million deal from the Atlanta Braves as a result of Seitz's ruling, but an overall free-agent system needed to be implemented. Miller opposed total, unrestricted free agency. As an economist, he knew that flooding the market with as many as 350 free agents every season would drive down salaries. Management first proposed 10 years of service to qualify for free agency. Polling his membership, Miller came up with six years, the standard in effect to this day. The new agreement permitting free agency was signed July 12, 1976.

Messersmith was not the last rotation mainstay the Dodgers would lose. Two years later, southpaw Tommy John was offered contracts by nine teams. The winning bidder was the Yankees, who quadrupled John's salary from the $72,000 he earned in Los Angeles.

The $1 million annual salary barrier was finally cracked in 1980 when the Houston Astros, the closest team to his Texas hometown, made free agent Nolan Ryan wealthy with a four-year deal.

The $1 million annual salary barrier was finally cracked in 1980 when the Houston Astros, the closest team to his Texas hometown, made free agent Nolan Ryan wealthy with a four-year deal, quadrupling his salary with the Los Angeles Angels. Ryan's departure was a move Angels owner Gene Autry regretted for the rest of his life.

"Gene was a man who if you were a person in charge of your area, that was your bailiwick," said then-Autry assistant John Moynihan. "Nolan Ryan asked [Angels GM Buzzy Bavasi] for $1 million after pitching four no-hitters for the Angels. Buzzy said he could get two players for $500,000 apiece. Gene told me he should have gone into Bavasi's office and told him to give Nolan the $1 million. He loved Nolan and hated to see him go to Houston, Texas. That was something that bothered him for a long time."

Despite the owners annually stumbling all over each other to snap up free agents, they succumbed to traditionalists' and conspirators' entreaties to control or even roll-back the tide of affluent players. Under commissioner Peter Ueberroth in 1985, the owners agreed to collude to clamp down on free-agent offers. The effort became a miserable failure once the courts got involved. Five years later, baseball had to pay a $280 million settlement to the players to make up the money they supposedly lost with the temporary dearth of contract offers.

Almost 40 years after the free-agency system began, teams have adopted new tactics to hold onto talent and save some dollars. Selected major leaguers are signed to long-term contracts early in their careers to keep them out of arbitration and the first couple of years of free agency. Concurrently, the big-league debuts of some top prospects are delayed a few weeks into the start of the season to avoid amassing the service time that would qualify them for free agency in six years. Salary caps have put some constraints on free agency in the NFL, NBA, and NHL. But the free marketplace operates unsullied in baseball—with the exception of a luxury tax imposed on the highest-spending teams. And it was all because of specific language in Paragraph 10-A that was never interpreted correctly for decades.

Bullpen Specialization

Building Baseball Backwards as the Bullpen Drives Pitching Strategy

Any opponent going up against the Kansas City Royals months before their startling World Series run in 2014 hoped to get a lead and hang on prior to the seventh inning. Otherwise, they were in trouble. The ultimate trio of bullpen producers, culminating four decades of game-changing transformation in the strategy of pitching, flashed firm red lights against rallies.

Kelvin Herrera in the seventh. Wade Davis in the eighth. Greg Holland to close. None of the trio had ERAs in 2014 higher than 1.44. Combined, they allowed just 29 earned runs all season. The threesome represented all teams' desire to construct their pitching staffs in a manner helped mightily along by Hall of Famer Tony La Russa and longtime sidekick Dave Duncan a generation before.

The rise of bullpen specialization represents the biggest in-game change since Babe Ruth transformed offense from dead-ball play to power play. Going hand-in-hand with the five-man rotation and stricter pitch counts, the rise of the pen has changed both pitching statistics and roster composition. Extra position players scrambled for jobs as teams began employing 12, and for short periods of time, 13 pitchers, finding with heavy use of the bullpen that even seven relief pitchers sometimes is not enough.

That's in stark contrast to pro baseball's first 100 years. Pitching was centered on starters who labored in sweat-soaked, heavy flannel uniforms in the late innings, trying to find their last bit of gas in the tank as savvy hitters calibrated the increasing hittability

Tony La Russa (center) with Nationals GM Mike Rizzo (left), one of countless execs who crafts his bullpen with La Russa's pioneering bullpen strategy in hand. Joining La Russa and Rizzo is top amateur coach Peter Caliendo.

Hall of Famer Goose Gossage (right) with
ex–White Sox player Pete War

of their stuff. The Hall of Famers and near-greats had a finishing kick, though, sometimes going deep into extra innings to complete what they started. In a 1961 complete-game, 13-inning win, Sandy Koufax threw 213 pitches.

Bullpens were repositories for failed or old starters.

"I was at the forefront where it really started to be more specialized," said Hall of Famer Goose Gossage, who spanned the era from early 1970s stretched-out closer to early 1990s defined bullpen roles. "We were used much differently back then. No one had really thought of building a ballclub [via the bullpen].

"You didn't want to go into the bullpen because it was a junk pile where old starters went who couldn't start anymore. You were not groomed for the bullpen like today."

Sometimes, the busiest and winningest hurlers often did double-duty as their teams' best relievers in between starts. When Dizzy Dean won 30 for the 1934 Cardinals, six victories came in relief. Ol' Diz appeared in 50 games, of which 33 were starts. He was just as busy the following two seasons: 1935, 50 games, 36 starts; 1936, 51 games, 34 starts. During that period, Dean recorded 23 saves, including a league-leading 11 in 1936. Even into the 1970s, a starter could be called upon to try to get a crucial out or two on his off-day. On June 3, 1971, in Cincinnati, the Cubs' Ken Holtzman tossed his second career no-hitter. Two nights later, on June 5 in Atlanta, manager Leo Durocher called upon southpaw Holtzman to face lefty pinch hitter Mike Lum in the 11th inning. Lum homered to win the game.

Some of the handling of the first generation of true closers was barbaric by today's standards. After abusing Koufax, Dodgers skipper Walter Alston was equally careless in 1974 with closer Mike Marshall, who claimed he could pitch every day because of his graduate studies in kinesiology. Marshall appeared in a big-league record 106 games over 208 $\frac{1}{3}$ innings, finishing 83 contests, for a 15-12 record and 21 saves. He'd go on to set the AL record with 90 games pitched in 1979.

Meanwhile, Durocher was equally old-school in handling sinker-baller/Vaseline-ball practitioner Phil Regan when he came over to the Cubs in a trade from LA in 1968. Later that season, on August 10, 1968, in Cincinnati, Regan pitched 3 $\frac{1}{3}$ innings for a win over the Reds in a Saturday night game. The next afternoon, Regan entered in relief of Holtzman in the seventh. He pitched 7 $\frac{2}{3}$ innings for his second win in a row, giving up a two-run tying homer to Johnny Bench and working through the 14th inning. The Cubs scored in the 15th. Still, starters dominated. Rotation-rich teams like the Athletics carried as few as nine pitchers in the early 1970s.

Subtly, the best managers began employing multiple relievers to set the table for their closers. While winning the first of three consecutive World Series in 1972, Dick Williams used sidearming righty Bob Locker and lefty Darold Knowles to bridge from starters to Hall of Fame closer Rollie Fingers. Former starter Joel Horlen appeared in 32 games in the '72 campaign. Williams used six other pitchers (besides his rotation), but none worked in more than eight games.

Subtly, the best managers began employing multiple relievers to set the table for their closers.

A further evolution wrapped up the 1970s. First Dick Tidrow, then Ron Davis served as seventh- or eighth-inning setup men for Gossage on the Yankees. Davis was 14-2 and 9-3 in that role his first two seasons in 1979 and 1980.

"Ron Davis used to make me feel guilty about my job," Gossage said. "It was easy. Having RD and doing what these [setup] guys are doing today, it's easy. I used to take shit from everybody. They did all the work. They were used in the seventh and eighth. That's as close to [today's schedule] as I've ever worked, but I still worked harder than how these guys are used today."

Eventually, Tony La Russa came upon today's formula in an attempt to revive the career of Dennis Eckersley, who had faltered as a starter. In his first Oakland season in 1987, Eckersley worked 115²/₃ innings, splitting closer duties (16 saves each) with Jay Howell. But in 1988, La Russa largely restricted Eckersley to the ninth inning. He worked 72²/₃ innings over 60 games with 45 saves.

"If we can get one great inning out of him, let him close, that's where 'closer' became a coined phrase," said Gossage.

La Russa chess-pieced Gene Nelson as his number one setup man to complement lefties Rick Honeycutt and Greg Cadaret, and righty Eric Plunk. All appeared in at least 49 games, but only Nelson averaged as much as two innings an appearance. Gossage took his turn in the changing cast of Eckersley setup men in 1992 with his last decent season.

The basics of the model modern bullpen had been cast. Add a LOOGY (left-handed one-out guy) and perhaps a top starting prospect breaking in slowly as a reliever, and you have the core of the game in the 2010s. Thus there are no firestorms when a Corey Kluber is pulled with 18 strikeouts and a lead after eight innings. Each manager has a well-stocked pen.

The Year of the Pitcher

Baseball Reverses 1968 by Tinkering with the Basics

Baseball usually makes changes at a glacial pace.

But when it's facing the bases loaded with no outs, the game will surprise you by how quickly it can adapt.

By 1968, baseball had been under fire for the better part of a decade for being too pedestrian and old-fashioned compared to the fast-paced and brutal—but telegenic—spectacle of pro football. And the game undercut its own appeal as pitching-friendly conditions resulted in a near-re-creation of the Dead Ball Era in the "Year of the Pitcher," featuring Bob Gibson's record-low 1.12 ERA and Carl Yastrzemski leading the American League with just a .301 average.

The answer was to tweak the game to promote more offense. Baseball would never again act to boost pitching at the expense of more action.

Rules and dimensions have been tinkered with since the sport first developed in the mid-19th century. The lords of the game deadened the baseball to hold down salaries after a massive hitting splurge in 1930 and the onset of the Great Depression deeply cut into attendance. Rarely, though, have the rules makers so frantically closed and opened the spigot as they did in the 1960s.

The first action took place going into the 1963 season, after an offensive upswing spurred by the first four expansion teams in modern baseball history the previous two campaigns. Baseball legislated an expanded strike zone to its literal limits, from the shoulders to the knees. Comparisons to the then-booming NFL, led by Vince Lombardi's

Bob Gibson's 13 shutouts and 1.12 ERA in 1968 spurred baseball to alert the mound and strike zone for more offense.

Green Bay Packers dynasty, also were a likely factor. The ostensible motivation was to speed up games so MLB could keep up with the football Joneses.

But if the expansion of the strike zone was aimed at quickening the pace, the end result was only something the game's aces and historians could truly appreciate. Scoring dropped by nearly 1,100 runs in the National League and nearly 600 in the American League. The bigger strike zone only made Sandy Koufax's job easier in a 1963 season in which he was 25-5 with a 1.88 ERA and 11 shutouts, topped by a Fall Classic–record 15-strikeout spree against the Yankees in Game 1 of a World Series the Dodgers swept.

Others shared in the '63 pitching bounty. Lefty Dick Ellsworth of the Cubs was 22-10 with a 2.11 ERA pitching in cozy Wrigley Field. No other Cubs pitcher has sported such a low ERA since World War II. The entire Cubs staff had an ERA of 3.08, second only to the Dodgers' sterling 2.85 team ERA. Meanwhile, 42-year-old Warren Spahn of the Milwaukee Braves was 23-7 with a 2.60 ERA—third lowest of his 360-victory career—while tying a career-high with seven shutouts.

American League scoring remained at the '63 low levels for the next four seasons with the 1967 White Sox pitchers outdoing the Koufaxian Dodgers with a 2.45 ERA. The NL had a brief offensive upsurge at mid-decade. Willie Mays's 52 homers in 1965 stood as the last season in a generation a big leaguer other than the Cincinnati Reds' George Foster—also with 52 in 1977—reached the vaunted 50 mark until the Detroit Tigers' Cecil Fielder's 51 in 1990. Offense disappeared baseball-wide in 1968. The AL's team ERA was 2.98. Paced by the Gibson-led Cardinals' 2.49, the NL's figure was just a tick higher at 2.99. Only three of the 10 NL teams slugged 100 homers or more. Six AL teams reached 100 taters, with the world champion Tigers

On the Pace of the Game

"Even baseball, the sportswriters' 'national pastime,' can be a slow-motion bore. Finger resin bag, touch cap, look for sign, shake head, shake again, check first, big sigh, wind up, finally pitch. Crack! Foul ball—and the fans could be halfway to Chicago by jet. Even a good thing palls when the games go on day after day for six months." —Time *magazine tribute to Vince Lombardi, 1962*

SPITBALLING

truly bucking the trend with 185. Danny Cater was second to Yastrzemski with a .290 average. Only two AL hitters had at least 100 RBIs, and only Willie McCovey had as many in the NL. Pitchers had unbelievable tough-luck records. The Cubs' Fergie Jenkins was 20-15, but lost five decisions by 1–0 scores. Pirates lefty Bob Veale was just 13-14 despite a 2.05 ERA.

Lack of pennant races made matters even worse. The Tigers won the AL by 12 games while the Cardinals waltzed in by a nine-game margin.

The owners had their hands full in the 1968-69 offseason. They dismissed out-of-his-league commissioner William "Spike" Eckert. For 1969, the moguls instituted two divisions in each league and a five-game League Championship Series. Despite the downslide in scoring and attendance, they locked in the game's second wave of expansion with NL teams in Montreal and San Diego and AL franchises in Kansas City and Seattle.

Boost the offense? The honchos had to do far more than juice the baseball. They reversed their 1963 actions, shrinking the strike zone from the top of the knees to the armpits. But more importantly, a basic playing condition was changed in a manner not seen since the 19th century. The mound was lowered from 15 to 10 inches (eight inches had originally been proposed). Coming off the rubber, pitchers now would work on a more gradual incline.

"To give perspective, if you're a hitter and I'm standing above you on a stepladder and I'm dropping the ball down on you vertically, that's virtually impossible to hit," said then–White Sox lefty Tommy John, whose 1.98 ERA ranked just fifth in the AL in 1968. "So now if I am standing horizontally with you and I'm throwing horizontally, that ball is the easiest ball to hit . . . [Lowering the mound] makes it easier as a hitter."

The bottom-line change reversed the offensive depression the next two seasons. By 1970, just two of the 24 teams—the Los Angeles Dodgers and Kansas City Royals—slugged fewer than 100 homers. The lowest team ERAs in '70 were the Baltimore Orioles at 3.15 for the AL and New York Mets at 3.45 for the NL. But teams feasting on inept expansion franchises had as much effect on the robust hitting numbers, as had happened in the first expansion wave in 1961-62. One beauty about baseball is that the game constantly re-adjusts itself. Hitters' performances slid downward again starting in 1971. The American League

By 1970, just two of the 24 teams—the Los Angeles Dodgers and Kansas City Royals— slugged fewer than 100 homers.

instituted the designated hitter starting in 1973. A semblance of balance was finally achieved later in the 1970s. But a new factor intruded into baseball as the 1990s concluded—use of performance-enhancing drugs that inflated power numbers as never before.

The Designated Hitter

The AL's Numbers Transform as the NL Stubbornly Holds Out

Only one significant difference remains between the American League and the National League. Interleague play, movement of players via free agency, and the July 31 trade deadline, umpiring crews servicing both leagues, and the end of the AL and NL presidencies and league offices have softened the formerly sharp league borders. Teams have even transferred between leagues. The Milwaukee Brewers moved to the NL in 1998. The Houston Astros, balancing out each league at 15 teams, switched to the AL and an intra-state rivalry with the Texas Rangers, in 2014.

Only the designated hitter provides a gulf—and a big one—between what used to be called the "senior" and "junior" circuits. The DH was instituted in 1973 by the AL, prompting a different, more robust style of offense and fewer chess pieces to move. Pinch hitting for pitchers, late-inning double switches, and the need for a substantial bench to service both strategies do not exist in the AL. Meanwhile, attempts to standardize the DH throughout the majors have been met with a roadblock as the NL has refused to add the extra hitter. The DH came about as part two of a post-1968 effort to inject more offense into baseball and counter mass-media hoopla over the NFL's faster pace and appealing brutality. Lowering the mound and compressing the strike zone immediately after '68's "Year of the Pitcher" was the first

Twins star Tony Oliva was one of a core group of star players who spent the bulk of the rest of their careers as designated hitters after the extra batsman was added in 1973.

effort. Experiments in forms of a "designated pinch hitter" had been undertaken in the minor leagues and in spring training as the 1960s drew to a close. But the lineups were status quo after the mound and strike zone adjustments for 1969. Aided by two weak expansion teams in Seattle and Kansas City, AL scoring per game increased 20 percent. Overall offensive numbers increased in 1970 with a peak of 8,109 runs and 1,746 homers, then declined in 1971 to 7,472 runs and 1,484 homers. A strike that wiped out the first week of the season in 1972 helped the numbers tumble further to 6,441 runs and 1,175 homers, finally prompting the adoption of the DH. The new DH was an instant protein jolt for the AL. Scoring jumped 23 percent, the best increase since 1911. Totals were 8,314 runs and 1,552 homers. The Yankees' Ron Blomberg carved a distinction in his journeyman career as the first DH on April 6, 1973, but more famous names occupied the position elsewhere in the AL. A score were refugees from the NL who were slow, aging, and/or best kept away from a defensive position. But these guys could still swing a bat: future Hall of Famers Frank Robinson, 37, with the Angels, and Orlando Cepeda, 35, with the Red Sox; Tommy Davis, 34, with the Orioles, and Deron Johnson, 35, with the Athletics. Master batsman Tony Oliva, 35, shifted to DH from the outfield for the Twins for the last four years of his career in 1973. Heavyweights Frank Howard and Gates Brown alternated at the position for the Tigers.

Tony Oliva before they took his glove away

In 1975, two more Cooperstown-bound NL alums—Hank Aaron and Billy Williams—joined the ranks of DHs in their first experience in the AL. Two extra seasons as DH in Milwaukee enabled Hammerin' Hank to finish with 755 homers. Williams was a somewhat unwilling DH when traded to Oakland from the Cubs. He had played 1,117 consecutive games from 1963 to 1970 at all outfield positions. "I told him I could still play [the field]," Williams said of Oakland owner Charlie Finley. "He said I don't want you to play. All I want you to do is maybe DH. The first year was exciting because I knew we had some great players [coming off three straight World Series]. I ended up with a good year. I had a lot of fun out there.

"But it's kind of hard. All those years I'm playing every day [in the outfield] I found after I hit, after I made an out or hit a home run, I went to the outfield. I'm out here, I have to catch a ball, it makes me a complete player. You have more to think about than just hitting a baseball. You're groomed in the NL that you're a complete player, throw people out, right position to catch a ball, you want to keep it until you take off the uniform."

Another NL refugee from the Reds, the Royals' Hal McRae, likely was the first position player to complete a successful adjustment to the DH to carve out the bulk of his career in that role. He'd go on to collect 2,091 hits and twice led the AL in doubles with a high of 54 in 1977.

"We were a better club if I was DH," McRae said of the Royals' speedy outfield. "I had to learn to stay in the game, number one . . . I ran in the tunnel [between at-bats]. I'd walk around in the tunnel listening to the radio or watch TV. We had a laundry basket in Kansas City and I'd push the basket to stretch my legs. If I broke a sweat, I tried to maintain a sweat."

Eventually the stigma of being a DH disappeared as converted position players booked passage to the Hall of Fame. Original middle infielder Paul Molitor was primarily a DH the last half of his 21-season career on his way to 3,319 hits and a .306 average with the Brewers, Blue Jays, and Twins. Injuries and immobility at first base enabled Frank Thomas to finish with 521 homers after shifting to primarily DHing starting eight years into a 19-season career. Near-future enshrinee Jim Thome likely amassed bonus time, playing until 42 and finishing with 612 homers, being able to DH after back issues made regular first-base duty problematic.

Eventually the stigma of being a DH disappeared as converted position players booked passage to the Hall of Fame.

AL pitchers had to work harder with the extra hitter. Where once a 4.00 ERA made a pitcher a borderline candidate for demotion, now it afforded him relative job security. Any moundsman under 3.00 was a league leader. Today, in the post-PED era, much of the NL struggles for depth in their lineups.

The debate over whether the DH should finally be used in the NL never ends.

"It's time to go to a DH all the time," Royals hitting coach Dale Sveum told the *Chicago Tribune* on May 30, 2015, while his team played an interleague game without the DH at Wrigley Field. "This is the first time all year our [pitchers] are going to hit. Two months into the season. We build our team around a DH, obviously. National League teams don't."

Even while banned from the NL, the DH is entrenched as a game changer.

Night Baseball

Games under the Lights Change Culture, Put Players on Entertainers' Hours

NO. 16

Nighttime baseball experiments at the amateur and minor-league levels date back to 1880, but illumination did not come to the majors until 1935. And eventually arc lights at every stadium—with Wrigley Field a quirky holdout until 1988—brought a change in the culture of baseball.

The modern game is basically a night-shift, 4-to-midnight operation with players putting in entertainers' hours. First, night baseball was meant to boost attendance, but now it's staged for the convenience of television audiences. Sunday day games—with doubleheaders long a thing of the past—no longer seem the top draw in the weekly attendance cycle. The present top draws are Saturday night contests, which can be packaged with eating and drinking in fans' "night out" routines.

Prior to the advent of night games, the daytime-only schedule upheld tradition, but was often bad for the bottom line. Afternoon baseball's attendance was held down by the typical workingman's six-day-a-week schedule. Teams had to goose the gate with the two-for-the-price-of-one attraction of doubleheaders on the typical fan's one weekly day off on Sunday. Season attendances of 1 million were not recorded until the 1920s, and then only by a handful of big-market franchises like the Yankees and Cubs.

The ravages of the Great Depression on attendance finally shed light on the logic of night baseball, via innovator Larry "The Raging Redhead" MacPhail, bossman of the Cincinnati Reds. With the Queen City's charter National League franchise one step ahead of bankruptcy, MacPhail persuaded NL owners to approve seven night games for the 1935 season.

The lights were an immediate hit during the first night game at Crosley Field in 1935.

MacPhail and Reds owner Powell Crosley invested $50,000 in a General Electric lighting system for Crosley Field with the goal of providing double the candlepower of the best-lit minor-league field. Engineers Earl D. Payne, Al Reuterer, and Charles Young set up the system, while Wayne Conover handled the calculations of the exact illumination power. The 632 Mazda lamps, each 1,500 watts, were mounted on eight light towers for their May 24, 1935, debut. MacPhail went all the way to the top to inject showmanship in the night game. President Franklin D. Roosevelt pressed a symbolic gold telegraph key in the White House to signal the switch to be thrown on the historic 2–1 Reds win over the Phillies.

But there was no rush to install lights elsewhere. MacPhail himself was the impetus for the second ballpark with lights—Brooklyn's Ebbets Field, where he moved as Dodgers president in 1938. On June 15 with the Reds as Dodgers opponents, Cincy's Johnny Vander Meer hurled his second straight no-hitter before 38,748.

Finally, the night-game breakthrough took hold from 1939 through 1941. Seventy night games were scheduled throughout the majors in 1940. The Athletics and Phillies took advantage of the illumination of their shared Shibe Park in Philadelphia, as did the Cardinals and Browns in co-habiting Sportsman's Park in St. Louis. Also taking their toe-dips in night baseball were the Pirates, Giants, Indians, and Senators. Other teams held out until after World War II, when attendance—boosted by returning veterans—skyrocketed. The Yankees and Braves lit up in 1946, the Red Sox in 1947, and the Tigers brought up the rear at Briggs Stadium in 1948.

Notice the one team missing in the chronicle of illumination. Beset by sagging attendance and declining team fortunes after the 1938 NL pennant, the Cubs planned to install lights for the 1942 season at Wrigley Field. Steel for the light towers was stored under the stands when the Japanese attacked Pearl Harbor on December 7, 1941. Owner Philip K. Wrigley donated the steel to the war effort, then backtracked several years later to ask the War Department for permission to install wooden light standards. He was denied. Wrigley never adequately explained why he did not proceed with lights after the war like other teams. The Friendly Confines remained the only day baseball holdout for 11 years after the owner's death in 1977. The Cubs' oddball afternoon-only status was a major factor in their unprecedented championship drought as the team likely suffered a form of "shift work disorder," with the physical drain of constantly switching from a 9-to-5-type schedule to the night-shift on the road, back and forth for six months, and the switch made worse flying to three road trips a season on the West Coast.

The All-Star Game began night-game play in 1967. The first World Series night game took place in 1971.

When the Wrigley-successor Tribune Company ownership finally installed lights after much community and political opposition, the first night game was scheduled for August 8, 1988 (8/8/88). The event was so unprecedented that more than 600 media credentials, a record at the time for a regular season game, were issued. Fittingly, the game was rained out in the fourth inning, and the actual first night game was not played until August 9 with NBC craftily having scheduled that contest for a national telecast.

Not all nights were ripe for baseball in the first few decades of lights. Sunday night games were frowned upon as a carryover from old blue laws, such as in Pennsylvania, where Sunday baseball was prohibited until 1931 and later a curfew ended Sabbath games early in the evening. The Houston Colt .45s had to ask permission from the NL to play on Sunday nights in 1962 to spare fans the brutal heat and humidity of day games at uncovered Colt Stadium, prior to the air-conditioned Astrodome's opening.

Despite a generation's worth of regular season night games, baseball still was a daytime-only sport for the World Series, tiebreaking playoff games, and the All-Star Game going into the mid-1960s. But NBC's first multi-year contract in 1966 packaging the Saturday Game of the Week with the World Series and All-Star Game provided for primetime telecasts on Memorial Day, July 4th, and Labor Day, the three national holidays during the regular season. The All-Star Game began night-game play in 1967. The first World Series night game took place in 1971. The 1970s saw NBC, then ABC presenting a regular schedule of Monday night regular season telecasts. Eventually the majority of postseason games, including all World Series and League Championship contests, were scheduled at night (or 5:00 p.m. on the West Coast for primetime airing in the East and Midwest) for the benefit of TV.

By the mid-2010s, slowpoke pitchers and count-working and fidgety batters often were thwarting baseball's attempts to modernize, inflating game times past three hours and losing younger fans who had to go to bed. Late and live wasn't always a good thing for baseball.

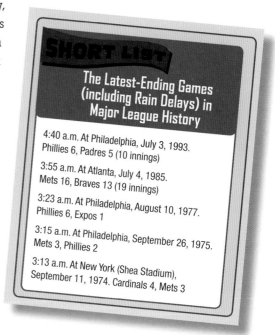

SHORT LIST

The Latest-Ending Games (including Rain Delays) in Major League History

4:40 a.m. At Philadelphia, July 3, 1993. Phillies 6, Padres 5 (10 innings)

3:55 a.m. At Atlanta, July 4, 1985. Mets 16, Braves 13 (19 innings)

3:23 a.m. At Philadelphia, August 10, 1977. Phillies 6, Expos 1

3:15 a.m. At Philadelphia, September 26, 1975. Mets 3, Phillies 2

3:13 a.m. At New York (Shea Stadium), September 11, 1974. Cardinals 4, Mets 3

Division and League Championship Series

Playoffs Get So Dramatic They Outshine the World Series

NO. **17**

Lagging behind the other pro sports as usual, baseball finally instituted playoffs, termed the League Championship Series, in 1969 after the second wave of expansion increased the count to 12 teams apiece in each league. The league lineups had been boosted to 10 each in the 1961 and 1962 expansions, but teams lollygagging in eighth, ninth or 10th place as August progressed couldn't sell tickets.

Fortunately, the entry of four expansion teams in 1969 made 12-team leagues far too unwieldy. Each league split into two six-team divisions, East and West, and best-of-five playoffs were instituted. Combined with adjustments to the strike zone and playing conditions to prevent another "Year of the Pitcher," the playoffs helped baseball better compete with the growing dominance of the NFL as America's preferred spectator sport.

Besides creating an elongated postseason, the playoffs have often become a main course instead of an appetizer to the World Series. The League Championship Series has often outshined the World Series in drama and memorable moments.

The Red Sox's "Idiots" celebrate after pulling off the greatest postseason comeback in baseball history during the 2004 ALCS.

And if the Division Series, by its comparative brevity, hasn't served as a tripwire for statistically dominant regular season teams upset by outwardly inferior clubs, then the LCS has served as the ultimate barrier to the promised land of the World Series.

The first three sets of LCSs went according to form from 1969 to 1971 with five of six series being clean sweeps by the more dominant regular season team. But in 1972, both the Oakland-Detroit and Pittsburgh-Cincinnati series each went the limit, with the latter going down to the final batter. Trailing 3–2 going into the bottom of the ninth of Game 5 at Riverfront Stadium, Johnny Bench tied the game with a homer off Pirates closer Dave Giusti. Two more singles off Giusti prompted Buccos manager Bill Virdon to summon right-hander Bob Moose, who got two outs. But with Hal McRae, later bound for heroics with the Royals, batting, Moose cast a wild pitch to send the Reds to the World Series. The game would turn out to be the last major-league contest in which Hall of Famer Roberto Clemente would play.

Fans had to wait just one year for the Reds to return to the NLCS to enjoy action that would put the new playoff on a par with the World Series for pure entertainment. The 99-win Cincinnatians dueled the nearly accidental NL East titlists, the New York Mets. At 82-79, the result of an out-of-the-blue 29-13 finish in which they climbed from last place in mid-August, the Mets had the lowest winning percentage of any first-place team in history up to that date.

The Mets were full of their comeback achievement and let opponents know as much. One of the chirpers was lithe shortstop Bud Harrelson. He had to be separated from offended Reds superstar Joe Morgan during batting practice before Game 3 at Shea Stadium. Bad feelings spilled into the game. Breaking up a double play, Pete Rose plowed into Harrelson. The ensuing brawl spread to both teams.

On Winning the American League Championship Series

"Not many people get the opportunity to shock the world. We came out and did it. You know what? We beat the Yankees. Now they get a chance to watch us on the tube." —*Kevin Millar, Boston Red Sox first baseman, after winning the 2004 ALCS from a 3–0 series deficit*

SPITBALLING

When the Reds took the field in the next inning, Rose was showered in left field with beer cans, batteries, and other garbage. Manager Sparky Anderson pulled his team off the field until cooler heads prevailed. The value of the LCS for unforgettable moments and as a stage for giant-killers was now established as the Mets went on to pull the playoff upset in five games before going on to nearly shock the defending champion Oakland A's in the World Series. New York took a 3–2 lead before the A's rallied to pull out the Fall Classic.

In 1976, the ALCS finally pulled even with the World Series for walk-off dramatics. The Pirates' Bill Mazeroski had been the only player to end a World Series with a homer against the Yankees in Game 7 in 1960. Now it was the New Yorkers' postseason walk-off turn. First baseman Chris Chambliss led

In 1976, the ALCS finally pulled even with the World Series for walk-off dramatics.

off the ninth of Game 5 against the Royals' Mark Littell with a homer that powered the Bombers into their first World Series in 12 years. Fans poured out onto the field.

Dramatic, and nearly improbable homers made the LCS must-viewing in the mid-1980s. First it was the Cardinals against shell-shocked Dodgers closer Tom Niedenfuer in Games 5 and 6 of the 1985 NLCS. Ozzie Smith, author of just 28 regular season homers in his 19 seasons, sliced a drive over the right field fence with one out in the ninth for a 3–2 Cards win in Game 5. Two days later, a real slugger, Jack Clark, lowered the boom against Niedenfuer with two out and two on in the ninth inning and the Dodgers leading 5–4 in Los Angeles. Clark's blast booked a trip to the World Series, where the Cards would fall.

Absolute king of desperate rallies was the ninth inning of Game 5 of the ALCS between the Angels and Red Sox in Anaheim in 1986. With a 5–2 lead in the ninth, a 3–1 lead in the series, and just two outs separating the Angels from their first World Series, starter Mike Witt served up a two-run homer to Don Baylor. Moments later with two out and a man on base, Witt was pulled in favor of closer Donnie Moore. Boom! Dave Henderson shocked the world with a two-run homer to give the Red Sox a 6–5 lead. Lost in the commotion was Rob Wilfong's RBI single in the bottom of the inning that tied the game, Henderson's 11th-inning sacrifice fly that eventually won it, and the Angels losing two more games to the Red Sox.

For a cumulative achievement, the 2004 ALCS showdown stands out. The Yankees had seemingly humbled their punching-bag Red Sox for the umpteenth time with a 3–0 series lead. Suddenly, the Red Sox were as loose as a collection of "idiots" could possibly be. They won four in a row—the only time in postseason baseball history a 3–0 lead was coughed up. All longtime Red Sox debts with the Yankees were settled in one fell swoop. Anything can happen, and baseball's annals are filled with powerful teams that stumbled in the multiple layers of playoffs.

The Wild Card

Baseball in September Becomes Meaningful Again

September 2011 ranks as the wildest, most entertaining finish in baseball history. Sixteen years after the wild card playoff berth was introduced, Yogi Berra's concept of "it ain't over 'til it's over" played out perfectly.

The Boston Red Sox fell out of first place in the American League East on September 2. They were still nine games ahead of the third-place Tampa Bay Rays at this point. Then, Boston really went south. Beset by clubhouse dissension and unprofessional player behavior, the Terry Francona–managed team stumbled to a 7-20 finish as the Joe Maddon–helmed Rays, enjoying a 17-10 September, caught them in the wild card race with three games to go. It would go down to the wire.

NO. **18**

The night of Wednesday, September 28, decided everything. In St. Petersburg, the Rays tied the Yankees 7–7 on a two-out, two-strike pinch-hit homer by Dan Johnson in the bottom of the ninth, then won the game in the bottom of the 12th on Evan Longoria's homer. Up in Baltimore, the Red Sox were one out from redeeming their September squandering with closer Jonathan Papelbon on the mound. Striking out the first two Orioles in the bottom of the ninth and trying to preserve a 3–2 lead, Papelbon gave up a double to Chris Davis. Then Nolan Reimold and Robert Andino proved every man with bat in-hand was dangerous. Reimold plated the tying run with a ground-rule double and Andino slashed a game-winning single, booking the Rays' trip to the postseason.

Three years later, on September 30, 2014, the Oakland Athletics felt confident of advancing in the postseason with a 7–3 lead going into the bottom of the eighth over the Royals at Kansas City's Kauffman Stadium. The A's had loaded up with starting pitching in

Only four years after the franchise's birth, the Florida—now Miami—Marlins celebrated their World Series title as the first team to win it all, in 1997.

July, surrendering top infield prospect Addison Russell to the Cubs in the process. Despite a Red Sox-ian late-season slump, the A's still made the postseason.

But then things started to happen. The plucky Royals, a throwback to speedy 1980s artificial-turf teams, used three singles, three stolen bases, a walk, and a wild pitch to close to 7–6 as starter Jon Lester was chased. More "small-ball" with a single, sacrifice, steal, and sacrifice fly tied the game against A's closer Sean Doolittle in the bottom of the ninth.

Oakland regained the upper hand on an Albert Callaspo pinch single for an 8–7 lead in the top of the 12th. But the Royals revved up their memorable postseason run in the bottom of the inning with an Eric Hosmer triple, Christian Colon single, a stolen base, and a Salvador Perez single for a 9–8 victory.

You can't beat fun at the ol' ballpark, thanks to perhaps the key innovation of the 1990s in baseball—the wild card.

The game had long ceded the final two months of the season to football. Once training camps began, football grabbed the primacy of fan and media attention, pushing baseball to secondary status in coverage unless a local team was in the pennant race. The rise of sports-talk radio in the 1990s made matters worse. Management edicts in many markets were "all football, all the time."

"Two more weeks, training camp starts. It's perfect," Landry Locker, producer of the Dennis and Freido show on ESPN Dallas, told WFAA.com in July 2015. Now, the wild card counteracts such attitudes, enabling baseball to catch up with all other professional sports. The NFL had allowed wild card teams to achieve the playoffs beginning in 1970.

Baseball traditionalists who opposed the wild card did not account for the late-season publicity beating. And they did not account for excellent teams timing their upsurges in the wrong year with another surging team edging them out. Take the 1993 San Francisco Giants, winners of 103 games in Dusty Baker's first managerial season, for example. The newly established powerhouse Atlanta Braves, beefed up in '93 with Greg Maddux's free-agent arrival, ran wild down the stretch to win 104 games. In 1954 a 103-victory

SHORT LIST

Baseball's Worst Records Qualifying for the Playoffs

50-53 (strike season): 1981 Kansas City Royals. Lost Division Series 3–0.

82-80: 2005 San Diego Padres. Lost Division Series 3–0.

82-79: 1973 New York Mets. Lost World Series 4–3.

83-78: 2006 St. Louis Cardinals. Won the World Series 4–1.

84-78: 1984 Kansas City Royals. Lost League Championship Series 3–0.

Yankees team finished eight behind the 111-win Cleveland Indians. That was only one of three 100-victory seasons for the Casey Stengel/Ralph Houk/Yogi Berra–managed Bronx Bombers dynasty of 1949 to 1964. From 1933 to 1992, a total of 19 teams finished second or worse with 95 to 99 victories.

There were multiple runner-up achievers on several occasions. In 1964, the White Sox and Orioles ended up with 98 and 97 victories, frustratingly behind the Yankees' 99 total. Then, in what Hall of Famer Goose Gossage called the "Beasts of the East" competition, the Red Sox and Orioles each won 97 in 1977, all for nothing in the end with the Yankees clinching the AL East with an even 100 triumphs. The AL East became by far baseball's strongest division with a pair of teams finishing in second and third with at least 90 wins in three different seasons between 1978 and 1983.

Bud Selig has never gotten the credit for pushing for a series of game innovations in the 1990s when he was acting commissioner. The wild card, implemented in 1995, is likely the best of them all. The full impact of the new playoff route finally emerged in 1997. The other '93 NL expansion team, the Miami Marlins, became the first wild card team to win the World Series, breaking the hearts of the Cleveland Indians, attempting to end their own long championship drought.

Bud Selig has never gotten the credit for pushing for a series of game innovations in the 1990s when he was acting commissioner.

The Marlins repeated their wild card feat in 2003, catapulting from a 3–1 deficit in the National League Championship Series against the Bartman Game–plagued Cubs, then upending the Yankees in the World Series. That was the middle of three consecutive World Series triumphs by wild card entrants after the Angels in 2002 and preceding the 2004 Red Sox. The wild card also enabled Madison Bumgarner to stand with the all-time World Series pitching greats as the Giants won their third World Series in five seasons in 2014.

Six other wild card teams reached the World Series, including the 2002 Giants in the first all–wild card matchup in the jewel event.

Now, with the format change requiring two wild cards to face each other in a one-game playoff, a bit of the old disappointment of those 100-win bridesmaids has re-entered the sport. Imagine to strive so hard through the grueling regular season, but then have all the good work undone via baseball's quirky breaks in a one-and-done game.

The good still outweighs the bad, though. Fewer teams will throw in the towel as early as the trading deadline, and the race to win as many games as possible now correctly permeates baseball's collective thinking.

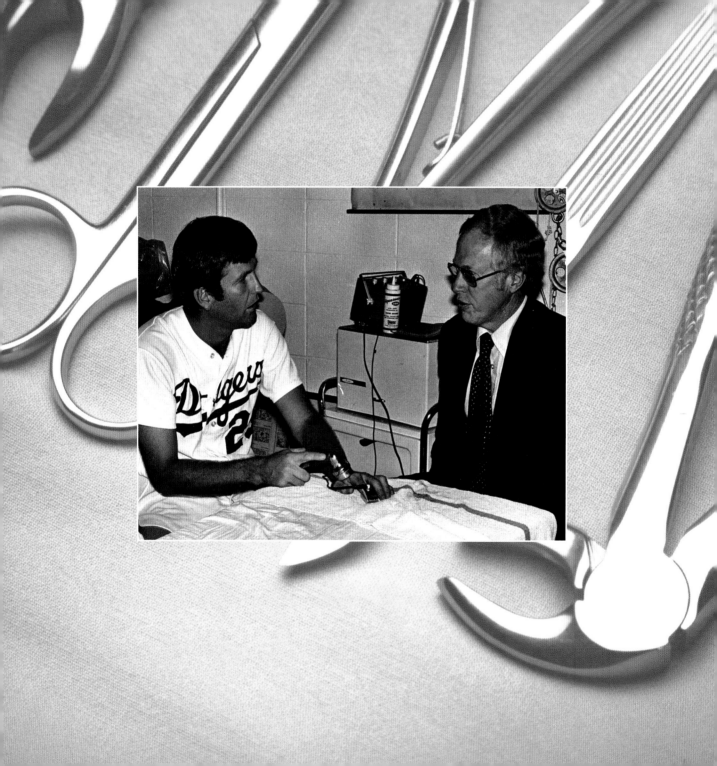

Tommy John Surgery
Getting Better Gas-Mileage Arms

The Six Million Dollar Man starring Lee Majors was filming its second ABC season in the summer of 1974 when Tommy John became baseball's surgical guinea pig.

John would get a no-mileage natural body replacement for a worn-down elbow thanks to the lefty pitcher's own courage and the ingenuity of a humble surgeon named Frank Jobe who was not afraid to go out on a limb. The end result has far outlasted Majors's show. "Tommy John Surgery" has changed the game of pitching, saving countless careers of both moundsmen and position players by transplanting healthy tissue to take the place of torn ulnar collateral ligaments.

The surgery that Jobe pioneered with John in '74 has been so refined that pitchers have thrown harder post-op than prior to the operation, while some teams sign recent surgical patients as free agents with the expectation that they'll recover to pitch within the next year.

Jobe did not stop with his trademark elbow surgery. His orthopedic breakthroughs extended to shoulders, such as the operation on Dodgers ace Orel Hershiser in 1990 that cut down trauma on tissue during the surgery. Such a feat should never be underrated since the ball-and-socket shoulder is even trickier to repair than the elbow.

Jobe had so much impact on baseball that John once told the *Orange County Register* that a Hall of Fame medical wing should be created starting with the surgeon as charter member. The pair got close to that goal. John appeared alongside Jobe when the latter was honored in a special ceremony at Cooperstown during the 2013 induction weekend.

Two years later, a new Hall of Fame inductee could credit Tommy John surgery for his

Tommy John (left) and Dr. Frank Jobe, who together pioneered
a surgical technique that has saved countless pitchers' careers

presence at the lectern. John Smoltz was one of scores of pitchers who had second life after the transplant procedure. Others included Ryan Dempster, Stephen Strasburg, Billy Wagner, David Wells, Kerry Wood, Matt Harvey, Brian Wilson, Chris Carpenter, A. J. Burnett, Tim Hudson, Francisco Liriano, and Joe Nathan.

Such a long record of success prompted a torrent of praise for Jobe. But that would never be matched by decades of paying-it-forward by the skilled doctor, who died at 88 in 2014. Mentored by pioneering sports-medicine practitioner Robert Kerlan in Los Angeles in the 1960s, Jobe launched the careers of a new generation of orthopedic specialists.

"He was one of the most modest people I've been around," said former Dodgers general manager Fred Claire, who depended on Jobe's diagnostic and surgical skills in his more than a decade at the LA helm.

"He was very, very humble. You would never hear him mention anything about accomplishments. He was proud of [Tommy John surgery's impact], but you would never hear him mention it, people he'd train, his contribution. It just wasn't who he was."

Jobe's operation had its roots in John's longtime balky elbow, which began barking as far back as the minor leagues in 1962. John said he took the first of 40 injections to battle pain and inflammation on November 22, 1963, and somehow carved out an effective career with the White Sox, then cross-country in Los Angeles after coming over in a blockbuster trade for Dick Allen late in 1971. He finally shredded the UCL on July 17, 1974, at Dodger Stadium.

Jobe first prescribed rest. That did not work. The good doctor then suggested a first-of-its-kind ligament transplant in which a tendon would be taken out of his right forearm to take the place of the bad ligament. Jobe previously had performed similar hand and wrist

On Frank Jobe the Mentor

"Another thing Frank did not get credit for was being a great, great mentor to young orthopedics. In spring training every year, he'd bring in the Jobe Fellows to serve two weeks in Dodgertown. Look at the chief orthopedic person of a number of teams, many were trained by Frank." —*former Dodgers general manager Fred Claire*

SPITBALLING

transplants. He was attempting to enter a brave new world to work on a pitcher who depended on twists and torque to get big-league hitters out. John urged Jobe to proceed.

"There was no doubt," John said in 2009. "People thought I laid awake at night anguishing over it. . . . I asked him to do it right now [August]. He said he had to schedule it, that [he wanted] as many brilliant minds in the operating room [as possible]. He said, 'I really don't know what I'm doing on this. I want other people in there I trust.'"

John's take on Jobe was the same as Claire's. "The minute a doctor tells you he is humble, that's the doctor I want operating on me," he said.

Surgery was scheduled for September 25, 1974, at Centinela Hospital in Inglewood, California. Jobe made no promises. But by mid-season 1975, John was recovering nicely. He made a full comeback in 1976, and racked up three 20-win seasons for the Dodgers and Yankees between 1977 and 1980, pitched through age 46 in 1989, and finished with 288 victories. He said he never again experienced elbow problems.

"There are a lot of pitchers in baseball who should celebrate his life and what he did for the game of baseball," John said after Jobe's death. But the true measure of Jobe's life went far beyond the career-saving surgery.

"Frank was very much the innovator. But he realized one thing: the importance of the trainer," Claire said. "Upon Frank's recommendation, we [the Dodgers] hired one of the first physical therapists. We were one of the first to hire an assistant trainer. While I was GM, I had one guideline: anything Frank asked for, he got." Jobe met Sandy Koufax late in the immortal's career, then dovetailed with him again when he was the Dodgers' roving minor-league pitching instructor under Claire and predecessor Al Campanis. The only regret was not having a forward-thinking medical mind nearly a decade earlier when Koufax's "Left Arm of God" was wracked by arthritis and other pain.

The good doctor then suggested a first-of-its-kind ligament transplant in which a tendon would be taken out of his right forearm to take the place of the bad ligament.

"He told me . . . had he been a better doctor and known more about the physiology of the body, I can almost guarantee you that Sandy Koufax needed Tommy John surgery," John said. "All of what Sandy had, all of his complaints [pointed to] Tommy John surgery. It was one of those things that he couldn't figure out."

Koufax still punched the express ticket to Cooperstown, and John miraculously pitched into middle age while future Koufax wannabes did not have to retire at 30. Patience and pure innovation became as important to pitching as the curveball and 60 feet, 6 inches.

The Curveball

"Uncle Charlie" Separates Baseball's Men from the Boys

No pitcher since the closing decades of the 19th century could afford to throw just one pitch. His arsenal had to include a slower breaking pitch along with the basic "hardball." On the other hand, the inability to adjust to and hit a curveball and all its variants is the major stumbling block for a hitter's success in the big leagues. If you know "Uncle Charlie" or a "yakker" is coming, you better be ready with your own variant of your swing to catch its break in the zone.

The development of the curveball family was profound, affecting the pitching styles of the American and National League, which took different tracks as a result. By the mid-20th century, the AL was known as a "breaking ball" league while the NL preferred good ol' country hardball. The distinctions have lessened somewhat with intermingling of the leagues due to increased player movement in the free-agent era, and a unified umpiring staff with arbiters working games in both leagues.

When baseball still was in essence fast-pitch softball in the pre–overhand delivery days, antediluvian pitchers experimented with curveballs. Arthur "Candy" Cummings is popularly credited with the curve's invention in the late 1860s. But like so many other apparent pioneers in the 19th-century game, Cummings may simply have refined earlier players' offerings.

First thought to be an optical illusion due to its break, the curveball was definitively demonstrated as three-dimensional reality in the 1870s. Fred Goldsmith displayed his version of the curve in Brooklyn in and around 1870. Pitchers Charles Hammond Avery of Yale and Joseph Mann of Princeton supposedly used the curve in college games in the

Bert Blyleven was rated as having the game's best curveball in a Hall of Fame career.

mid-1870s, with Mann reportedly perfecting the pitch by throwing it in the hallways of his dormitory.

As the curve became established in early pro baseball, pitchers began trying to improve on its original concept. They came up with the basic sinker, and found that foreign substances or cuts in the ball's hide could affect its break. And while the spitball was only legal until 1920, pitchers found a way to force a quick break via the stress-inducing slider. Then came a forkball that seemingly broke straight down, eventually morphing via 1970s closer Bruce Sutter into the split-finger fastball. A select group of pitchers learned to make the ball dance its way to the plate via the knuckleball, and then hybrids of the flutterball and curve came together in the knuckle-curve first popularized by 1970s right-hander Burt Hooton.

Yet another hybrid brought the fantasy of the wood-repelling substance from the 1949 comedy *It Happens Every Spring* to superstation-borne reality on May 6, 1998. The Cubs' Kerry Wood employed a combo slider-curve, for want of a better term, to strike out 20 Houston Astros at age 20 at Wrigley Field. The pitch was simply unhittable, darting away from and under bats as if the repelling gel had been applied. Wood's monster took too much out of his arm, though. When he underwent Tommy John surgery 10 months later, he agreed to junk the pitch in favor of a more conventional breaking ball.

In the end, nothing freezes or tricks hitters like the original curve.

"I got about 60 percent of my 3,701 strikeouts on curveballs," said Hall of Fame right-hander Bert Blyleven, regarded by many hitters as the best curveball pitcher of his generation. "I could throw two fastballs and strike them out with my curveball. My fastballs set up my curveball. I didn't throw 100 mph like Nolan [Ryan], but I was in the 90 to 93 range with a little bit of movement, working the count in and out. When I needed a strikeout pitch, here comes the curveball and you got to beat me with that thing." Bill Melton, the 1971 AL home-run champion with the White Sox, said "the best curveball I ever faced was Blyleven's."

In the end, nothing freezes or tricks hitters like the original curve.

A Hall of Famer's great curve begat another Hall of Famer's. In this case, perhaps the greatest lefty of all time employing his sharp-breaking pitch switching off with his high-90s fastball fired the imagination of the youthful Blyleven, listening on KFI-Radio while growing up in Orange County, California.

"I learned my curveball by visualizing, listening to Vin Scully describing Sandy Koufax's pitch, which back then was called a 'drop,'" said Blyleven, now a Minnesota Twins TV announcer. "They had that 20-inch mound and he had that angle."

Nolan Ryan was best known for his century-quality heater, but also swooped in with the curve for some of his record 5,714 strikeouts. The pitch was at home in his two stints in the AL, as a young veteran in the 1970s with the Los Angeles Angels and to close it out as a celebrated baseball elder in the 1990s with the Texas Rangers. Meanwhile, Blyleven spent all but three seasons of his 22-year career in the AL.

"The art of pitching then was off-speed, get the guy off-balance," said Melton. "That's what we faced all the time. Even when they were behind you, they kept you off-balance. The AL was curveball league, the NL was fastball. I used to talk to Dick Allen, and he asked, 'They ever throw any fastballs here? In the NL, they used to challenge you, challenge you.'"

All breaking pitches invoke stress on the arm. Every youth coach cautions teenage pitchers to not throw a curve until they are fully developed physically, usually by the middle of high school. But Blyleven said the curve thrown with the proper mechanics should not cause arm problems.

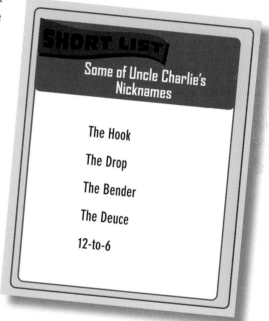

SHORT LIST

Some of Uncle Charlie's Nicknames

The Hook

The Drop

The Bender

The Deuce

12-to-6

"It's less stressful," he said. "The curveball to me is more the upper part of your right arm, the muscles up on top as you release the ball rather than a fastball or high slider, which is more the ligament area."

The curve could always be relied upon when the fastball was losing steam later in the game. "You can get guys out if you throw 95, 97 mph with a split finger," said Melton. "But you're only going to go five, six innings. It's all hard, hard, hard."

Ah, if the coaches only had more patience. Blyleven said they'd reap the benefits if they didn't quickly re-direct pitchers with wanderlust curves to throw more control-oriented sliders instead. Something about a mastered curve seems so basic, so traditional.

Instant Replay
Righting a Century-and-a-Half Worth of Wrongs

The images are as everlasting as those of Babe Ruth pointing, Bobby Thomson swinging, or Jackie Robinson sliding safely around Yogi Berra at home plate.

The full-color moving images, analog in 1985 and digital in 2010, show Don Denkinger and Jim Joyce, respected veteran big-league umpires, blowing calls at first base that arguably cost a World Series for the St. Louis Cardinals in the former instance and definitely cost a perfect game for Armando Galarraga in the latter.

Umpires are human and make mistakes. They admit error, too, and have done so to the players and managers affected since the start of the game. But there was no appeal or recall. A decision rendered is a decision imprinted in the books.

Yet for about 35 years from the mid-1960s onward, an increasingly sophisticated video instant-replay system on big-league telecasts has been laying the arbiters' errant calls bare for the whole world to watch. Starting with simple playback of the original live televised image, moving on to multiple isolated angles used for the Denkinger out-of-position decision in Kansas City and finally crystal clear high-definition images for Joyce's too-quick call in Detroit, replays have increased the second-guessing throughout baseball.

Tradition and the desire to retain the human factor prevailed, though, with baseball only toe-dipping into replay in a new millennium, falling "20 years behind the NFL," in the words of former top referee Jerry Markbreit. Nothing changed until a tipping point of nakedly blown calls during the 2012 postseason was reached. Baseball could not resist any longer the replay wave that had long washed over all other pro sports.

NO. 21

Comcast SportsNet Chicago's replay equipment in its control truck affords most of the angles seen by umpires considering reversals of calls in New York.

On One's Own Missed Call in the World Series

"Well, I am in too close. I looked up, and I saw him catch the ball. And when I looked down I saw [Orta's] foot on the bag, and I called him 'Safe!' That amount of time that it took me to look down, because I was in so close, permitted me to miss it."
—*Umpire Don Denkinger, on his call that arguably cost the St. Louis Cardinals the 1985 World Series*

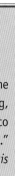
SPITBALLING

The combination of technology permitting up-close-and-crystal-clear images and embarrassment has stretched out gametimes and created some pregnant pauses in action while replays are reviewed in New York. But the old admonition to "get the call right" is being fulfilled, and the game will forever be better for the creeping modernity of both replay machines and attitudes.

The resistance to anything more than replays of "boundary plays"—like whether balls had cleared the fence or stayed in for a ground-rule double—was stiff. Even in the days after Joyce won friends and influenced people for his classy apology to Galarraga for costing him baseball immortality, no appetite for expanding replay existed from baseball commissioner Bud Selig on down to most players. The common theme was to keep the human factor, even with inevitable errors. One high team executive said differing stadium dimensions, preventing standardized camera positions for every potential angle, was a hindrance to expanded replay.

All the while, replays had long been accepted elsewhere in sports. Markbreit had long taught his referee trainees to handle the video interruptions in the NFL. During the Chicago Blackhawks–Philadelphia Flyers Stanley Cup Finals in 2010, soon after the Joyce-Galarraga fateful meeting, multiple players endorsed replays as a necessary help in the game. Sure enough, Patrick Kane's bad-angle overtime goal that won the Cup for the Hawks was confirmed by an overhead replay shot in a manner that other angles could not pin down.

Then came the umpiring mistakes in the 2012 postseason that left fans talking more about the calls than the game action, according to baseball operations chief Joe Torre, a veteran of a few beefs against the arbiters as a catcher, first and third baseman, and manager of a mini–New York Yankees dynasty.

Interestingly, a system of manager challenges similar to what has in fact been instituted was suggested by Galarraga back at the end of the 2010 season. The affable right-hander proposed each manager get two replay requests during a game.

No one suggests electronic review of balls and strikes. Not a soul is suggesting umpires can be replaced by a kind of robot working off a "PitchTrax" electronic strike zone, a basic version of which is used to confirm pitches for the viewer on many baseball telecasts. Still, the debate rages on about whether replay has reached its limits, even among workmates.

Said Sarah Lauch, 14-time Emmy Award–winning producer of Comcast SportsNet Chicago: "That can only be a positive. Replays can only help the umpires because they don't have to take so much heat. The amount of angles they see is insane."

Working with Lauch is fellow producer Ryan McGuffey, recipient of five Emmys: "You can only go so far. I don't think you want too much replay. Kind of what it is now. If you're taking the human element out of the game, I don't think it's worth it."

And one thing never changes in baseball. Knowing what we know now, we cannot retroactively go back to right the wrongs, even with the testimony of those involved.

Take the view from 25 years later from Denkinger, relayed to ESPN's Mike Fish. He admitted he was out of position when he ruled the Royals' Jorge Orta had beaten Jack Clark's flip to closer Todd Worrell, covering first. And even in 1985, Denkinger sought to confirm his call off replays that were of inferior video quality compared to a generation later. He recalled going to the locker room afterward to query then-commissioner Peter Ueberroth about what he had witnessed on TV.

"I immediately asked him if I got it right or wrong, because up to that point I didn't know," Denkinger said. "He said, 'No, I don't think so. I don't think you got it right.' You just get that sick feeling."

Such emotions aren't prevalent today. The only complaints center on the total time taken for replays and the concept of interruptions. The concept of review has quickly won acceptance. If the age-old heated, but entertaining, argument between manager

If the age-old heated, but entertaining, argument between manager and umpire has to be sacrificed, so be it.

and umpire has to be sacrificed, so be it. The fans may have gone wild watching Lou Piniella heave the base into right field or Lloyd McClendon try to carry the base with him into the dugout. Great video, but in the end, the object is to get the call right by any legitimate means.

So why were umpires, whose calls can be confirmed, and players, who have yet another right of appeal that was formerly limited to baseball labor-laws, so resistant over the decades? Baseball accepts change, but only grudgingly, with a lot of unnecessary kicking and screaming.

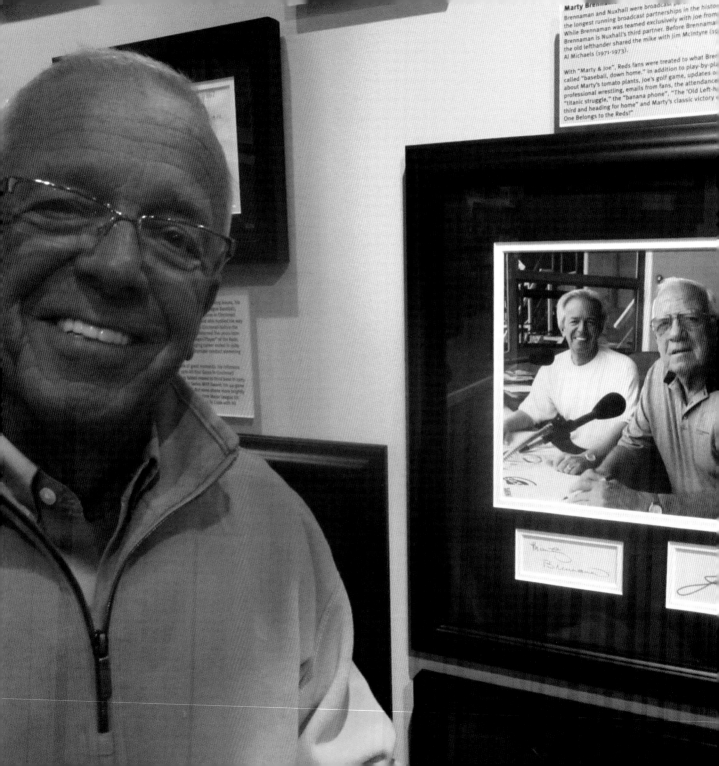

Radio
Baseball Reaches Far-Flung Fans

Like an electronic pied piper, radio ventured into what was then called the "ether," traversing all the small towns and farms, to bridge the distances and grab fans for baseball.

On the receiving end of the piper's baseball song were glowing, tube-filled receivers often constructed like living-room furniture. Fans hung on every word of announcers who prided themselves on precise diction. Now the baseball fan could hear his heroes in real time, live, with no gap in conveying drama. The stories poured into the media centers of men sitting around the cracker barrel—and the radio—in the rural general store, or the farmer placing the battery-operated receiver at the end of his plowing turn, tethered by effective radiated power to the drama of Major League Baseball.

NO. 22

Such was the game changer of radio, the first of the electronic media, bringing baseball to the masses while personalizing it in a way never possible by box scores or even newspaper photographs. Even in the darkest days of the Great Depression, when near-empty ballparks populated the game, the fans were no farther away than their radio sets. Move the clock forward to many urban neighborhoods in the Northeast and Midwest, where one could walk down the street and not miss a pitch of action by the mass of radios heard through open windows. A cousin of that phenomenon was found starting in 1958 at the Los Angeles Coliseum, then Dodger Stadium, as Vin Scully's airborne voice was heard throughout the stands by scores of fans wielding transistor radios.

"I think as long as the game is played, there's going to be a major place for radio," said Reds radio voice Marty Brennaman, among the Top Five big-league announcers in seniority in 2016. "Over and above all the other sports professionally and collegiate, there's never been a better marriage between a sport and a medium than there has been for baseball and radio.

Reds announcer Marty Brennaman with a photo of his beloved late broadcast partner Joe Nuxhall at the Green Diamond Gallery in Cincinnati.

"Radio is still the most mobile medium there is," the Hall of Fame broadcast-wing member continued. "As much as we have TV to carry [all the sports], it's still not as mobile as radio. People in their cars, truckers with 16-wheelers, whoever it might be. You can go about your daily business, in and out of your car, you can still hear baseball."

In the late 20th century, a fan could perfect the art of tuning into the majority of big-league games at night if, say, he were stationed in the Midwest or Middle South and was expert at twisting his dial to the 50,000-watt clear channel blowtorches synonymous with major-league baseball. With the Cubs playing on the road at night, he could count on them on WGN, the White Sox on WMAQ or WBBM, the Cardinals on KMOX, the Twins on WCCO, the Reds on WLW, the Tigers on WJR, the Indians on WWWE (now WTAM), the Rangers on WBAP, the Astros on WOAI, the Pirates on KDKA, the Braves on WSB, and the Phillies on WCAU. Starting in 1993, he could add the Rockies on KOA. On the right night, he could hear the majority of big-league games through the crackle of the radio boomers' sky waves.

These golden-throated announcers in many ways became the voices of the franchise via their storytelling talents and play-by-play styles.

Decades later, into a new millennium and with the media in turmoil due to the Internet, some of the 50,000-watt boomers have dropped baseball in favor of talk. But the far-flung radio networks for each team largely remain, giving small-city outlets a piece of the big-league pie.

And while the fans intently followed their favorites' feats over the frequencies, they also fell in love with the conveyors of the message. These golden-throated announcers in many ways became the voices of the franchise via their storytelling talents and play-by-play styles that ranged from rabid homer to down-the-middle reporter, depending on the region of the country.

"Consider the number of people who bring their headsets to the game," said the late Milo Hamilton, like Brennaman a Cooperstown broadcasters' member. "The number of people who turned down the sound on TV because they want to hear the radio version. They want to look at the picture, but they want more from the radio announcer than the TV announcer gives them. They'd rather know more about the picture than they would about stats."

Hamilton's own journey lasted more than a half-century. His radio resume includes the Cardinals, Cubs (twice), White Sox, Braves, Pirates, and Astros.

"I think when he's doing the games year after year, he becomes associated [with the image of the team]," Hamilton said. "I know I used to get mail—they thought I was the general manager. Why you didn't trade this, why you didn't trade that, all the things they counted on the radio announcer."

And the voice often ends up more memorable in the long run than all but his team's superstars. Sometimes the play-by-play man's pairing with a beloved color announcer or second voice is as big as the team itself. Such was the case in many seasons with Brennaman and sidekick Joe Nuxhall, the youngest-ever pitcher in the majors (at 15 in 1944) and the ultimate local-boy-made-good. None of their local TV counterparts could ever compare with the "Marty and Joe" show. "Developing personalities is much more difficult in TV than radio," said Brennaman, whose 1974 big-league debut with the Reds included calling Hank Aaron's 714th homer. "The medium is visual. There's much more down time, there's more silence because the visual aspect takes over. In radio, the play-by-play guy and whoever his partner is are constantly on the air. Having made that statement, in 10 or 12 years, let's see how many guys in our profession, broadcasting major-league baseball on TV only, go into the broadcasters' wing of the Hall of Fame."

That announcers' wing possesses a surfeit of talent, to be sure. First among equals, though, is Scully.

"I feel Vin is the best ever," Brennaman said of the broadcast poet who logged his 67th season in the Dodgers booth in 2016.

Interesting how Scully could only be heard in part of the Los Angeles market in 2015 having switched over to video years back, and thus consigned to a Time Warner cable network not picked up by many other regional cable providers. Had Scully stayed in radio as his primary outlet, his entire game broadcasts would have been heard throughout the Southland. In 2015 Scully was heard via a radio simulcast of his first three innings.

Indeed, in a video world of hand-held devices, radio still goes where moving pictures can't.

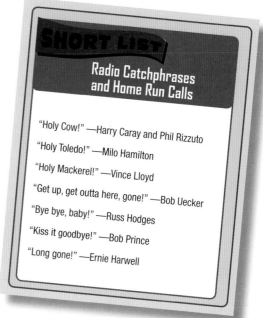

SHORT LIST

Radio Catchphrases and Home Run Calls

"Holy Cow!" —Harry Caray and Phil Rizzuto

"Holy Toledo!" —Milo Hamilton

"Holy Mackerel!" —Vince Lloyd

"Get up, get outta here, gone!" —Bob Uecker

"Bye bye, baby!" —Russ Hodges

"Kiss it goodbye!" —Bob Prince

"Long gone!" —Ernie Harwell

West Coast Baseball

Migration to the Pacific Shore Makes the Game National

NO.

23

For the first eight decades of professional baseball, the game was really a northeastern enterprise. Old industrial cities like Philadelphia, Boston, and St. Louis each had two teams. Outposts in both leagues were connected by part-day train travel. Fans in the South and the vast expanse west of the Mississippi had only their minor-league clubs as physical tethers to big-league franchises.

Even the first three postwar franchise moves failed to expand baseball's footprint. The Boston Braves moved in 1953 to Milwaukee, just 90 miles north of MLB stalwart market Chicago. The Philadelphia Athletics slid the baseball western boundary just a few hundred miles to Kansas City in 1955. But the A's new home was in the same state as traditional St. Louis, which lost its second franchise, the financially and competitively impoverished Browns, to Baltimore in 1954.

The true game changer took place in 1957 when the Giants, then the Dodgers, decided to flee their New York and Brooklyn bases, respectively, for San Francisco and Los Angeles.

A West Coast presence for baseball in the train-travel era would have made a 154-game schedule impossible. Airline travel in the pre-jet era was also relatively pokey with a flight from the Midwest to the West Coast taking seven hours. In 1951, *Collier's* magazine, projecting ahead to the world of 1960, referred to Jackie Robinson as manager of the decade-in-the-future Brooklyn Dodgers. There was no thought of greener pastures. But 1950s' population growth that tilted westward finally was the tipping point for baseball planting its flag on the West Coast.

The Dodgers and White Sox before one of three 1959
World Series games at the Los Angeles Coliseum

World Series victories in 1954 for the Giants and 1955 for the Dodgers failed to ensure long-term prosperity for either New York franchise. Brooklyn owner Walter O'Malley first cast around for a new stadium in the downtown part of his borough. Los Angeles city administrators then began sniffing around the Dodgers' availability. More New York political machinations ensued into 1957, but O'Malley and Giants owner Horace Stoneham were greasing their way out of town behind the scenes.

O'Malley ended up laughing all the way to the bank. While shoehorning a baseball diamond into the football/Olympics-designed Los Angeles Coliseum and drawing three crowds of more than 92,000 for Games 3 to 5 during the 1959 World Series, O'Malley benefited from a sweetheart deal for sparkling Dodger Stadium.

"There was so much excitement of the Dodgers coming to Los Angeles," said former Dodgers general manager Fred Claire, who celebrated his 24th birthday in the Coliseum pressbox as a sportswriter covering Game 4 of the 1959 World Series. "Where they were going to play and where they did play almost became incidental to the fact they were here. Vin Scully became an immediate hit and an educator of the fans who weren't familiar with the majors. It was a perfect scenario for their introduction. When the team got into the World Series in '59, it sent everything through the roof."

Dodger Stadium was carved into Chavez Ravine a short distance north of downtown Los Angeles. The sparkling new ballpark, which has aged well, drew 2.7 million in its first season in 1962 and set the stage for O'Malley to become first among equals in National League owners for the next two decades.

On 93,000 fans' May 7, 1959, tribute to Roy Campanella at Los Angeles Coliseum:

"All had candles. I had never seen anything like that in my life. Every one of us in that stadium had a candle. The lights went out and the light came on from all those candles. Christ Almighty, never seen anything like that in my life. I don't have words for that." —*John Moynihan, one-time Coliseum usher*

SPITBALLING

Meanwhile, Stoneham was far less successful in San Francisco. He ended up with the polar opposite of Dodger Stadium in Candlestick Park, placed on a windswept outcropping in San Francisco Bay. Reaching just one World Series in 1962 with five Hall of Famers in Willie Mays, Willie McCovey, Orlando Cepeda, Juan Marichal, and Gaylord Perry, the Giants suffered from chilly weather in night games at Candlestick along with winds that played havoc.

Giants attendance took a big dip after 1971, dropping into the low 500,000 range in 1974-75, and the Giants perennially seemed to have one step out of town to markets like Tampa Bay. Long-term stability in San Francisco was only achieved through the new ownership of Peter Magowan in the early 1990s and the construction of perennially sold out AT&T Ballpark.

Long-term stability in San Francisco was only achieved through the new ownership of Peter Magowan in the early 1990s and the construction of perennially sold out AT&T Ballpark.

The Dodgers were joined in Los Angeles by an AL expansion team in 1961. Cowboy star Gene Autry, at first only in the market for the team's broadcast rights for his KMPC radio station, ended up as owner of the Angels, taking the name of one of the city's two predecessor Pacific Coast League franchises. The Angels shared Dodger Stadium from 1962 to 1965 before relocating to new Anaheim Stadium in 1966.

Just like the Giants, the Athletics' tenure in the Bay Area has been bumpy. As the second franchise enduring a second move following the Braves' jump to Atlanta, the A's often have struggled to draw fans to Oakland Coliseum. Owner Charlie Finley's penury amid three straight World Series winners from 1972 to 1974 did not help. For years, the A's have tried to move to San Jose, in Giants territory, from their outdated ballpark, which bottomed out with sewage backup in recent years. The '69 expansion Seattle Pilots went bankrupt and were transferred to Milwaukee just before the 1970 season to be re-christened the Brewers under the new ownership of future commissioner Bud Selig. The expansion San Diego Padres, enduring a financial and competitive depression, seemed ticketed for Washington, DC, before McDonald's impresario Ray Kroc forged a moderate revival as owner. The Padres did make the World Series in 1984 and 1998, but got on really solid ground only after new Petco Park opened in 2004.

Meanwhile, the AL assuaged Seattle's injured feelings at the Pilots' failure by placing yet another expansion franchise, the Mariners, in the city in 1977. The Mariners slogged along as an AL bottom-feeder, prompting yet more franchise relocation reports, until 1995, when a stirring playoff run established the M's as a competitive franchise. The team's sudden success paved the way for construction of the spacious, retractable-roofed Safeco Field.

The game has certainly been better for planting its flag on the West Coast.

Expansion Teams

Painful at First, but Ultimately Good for the Game

Rooting for a stumblebum team losing 110 or even 120 games ain't much fun—just ask an original fan of the 14 expansion teams since 1961. Expansion franchises stocking themselves with talent were forced to take the game's leftovers and ne'er-do-wells.

And yet in the long run, brand-new teams proved a boon, certifiable game changers, breaking baseball's 16-team, eight-to-a-league mold that had existed since 1901 while extending the majors into new markets.

A spur to the first wave of expansion was baseball's ever-vigilant watch on keeping its exemption from the Sherman Anti-Trust Act. Talk was rife at the dawn of the 1960s of a third big league, the Continental League, backed by baseball mahatma Branch Rickey. The initial expansion package for 1961-62 included a National League team for New York, christened the Metropolitans. Los Angeles also locked down an American League team—named the Angels after the city's longtime Triple-A team—thanks to LA's market size and the initial attendance success of the Dodgers. Washington, DC, quickly got a replacement AL franchise for the longtime doormat Senators, relocated to Minneapolis. Houston's rapid growth lured an NL team, originally named the Colt .45s before being re-christened the Astros in their new domed stadium in 1965.

The Angels were run by "Cowboy" Gene Autry, who was recruited by the American League in 1960 to own the expansion franchise. Autry originally sought only the Angels' radio rights for KMPC-Radio, his Los Angeles outlet.

Founding Angels owner Gene Autry, his trademark hat showing why he was affectionately called "The Cowboy"

"Autry loved baseball," said John Moynihan, his one-time personal assistant with the Angels. But for all their efforts on behalf of the popular owner, the team never reached the World Series until four years after his death in 1998.

"The ballplayers used to say, 'Let's win one for the Cowboy,'" recalled Moynihan. "That was their whole thing. They wanted to win one for Gene Autry." Although the Mets suffered their record 120-loss inaugural season while being amused by manager Casey Stengel's colorful quotes and dugout naps, ownership under Joan Whitney Payson presided over a scouting department and farm system that helped stock the 1969 Mets, the first expansion team to win the World Series.

Eccentric ballparks welcomed the next batch of expansion franchises in 1969. The Expos played in 28,000-seat Jarry Park in the middle of a city recreational complex. Visiting Pirates slugger Willie Stargell aimed his moon shots at a swimming pool beyond the right field fence. The plate faced westward, so some games were briefly delayed as the setting sun over the left field bleachers blinded first basemen, who could not easily see teammates' throws. Still, the rickety ballpark promoted a festive atmosphere, and fans turned out despite 1969's 110 losses.

A contrary atmosphere was found in Seattle. The Pilots were forced to play in 1938-vintage Sick's Stadium, which only had 17,000 seats available on Opening Day. The stadium was later expanded to 25,000, but drawbacks like late-game lack of water pressure and obstructed views for both fans and announcers made the operation a travesty. The franchise went bankrupt anyway and was moved to Milwaukee to become the Brewers just before the 1970 season.

The replacement Senators became the second expansion team to move. Three financially troubled ownerships resulted in the franchise transfer to Arlington, Texas, to become the Rangers in 1972.

Also hurting were the San Diego Padres, whose mustard-and-brown uniforms were some of the ugliest in baseball history. Small crowds at then–San Diego Stadium lightened owner C. Arnholt Smith's pocketbook. Rumors were rife by 1973 that the franchise was headed to Washington, DC. But the Padres were saved for the city when McDonald's impresario Ray Kroc, frustrated in his attempt to buy his hometown Cubs, purchased the team.

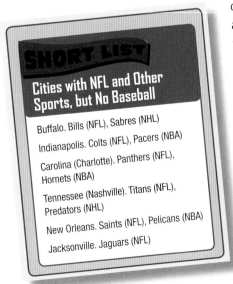

SHORT LIST

Cities with NFL and Other Sports, but No Baseball

Buffalo. Bills (NFL), Sabres (NHL)

Indianapolis. Colts (NFL), Pacers (NBA)

Carolina (Charlotte). Panthers (NFL), Hornets (NBA)

Tennessee (Nashville). Titans (NFL), Predators (NHL)

New Orleans. Saints (NFL), Pelicans (NBA)

Jacksonville. Jaguars (NFL)

The best-managed of the early expansion franchises was the Kansas City Royals. Run by dynamic owner Ewing Kauffman, the Royals won 88 games in their fifth season in 1973, captured three consecutive AL West titles from 1976 to 1978, played in the World Series in 1980, and won everything, aided by umpire Don Denkinger's bad call, in 1985. The Toronto Blue Jays then improved on the Royals' blueprint as one of the two AL expansion franchises in 1977. Toronto would go on to pace the American League East in a down period for the Yankees, and became the first expansion team to win multiple World Series.

The best-managed of the early expansion franchises was the Kansas City Royals.

The other '77 AL expansion team, the Seattle Mariners, were not as swiftly successful. The M's required the better part of two decades to develop a contender. The tide began to turn when they snared Ken Griffey Jr. in 1987, drafting first due to their consistently poor finishes. They reached the playoffs four times in the 1990s and early 2000s, and they were better than anyone else in regular season AL history with 116 wins in 2001.

Baseball expanded to Florida in 1993 with the NL's Miami Marlins and 1998 via the Tampa Bay Devil Rays (later changed to just Rays) of the AL. The concept seemed sound at first, given Florida's outwardly booming condition. Tampa Bay had previously tried to snare the White Sox and Giants. But when looked at under a microscope, the moves were flawed. Both the Marlins and Rays had mediocre stadium situations—the Marlins in a football park and the Rays in the ugly Tropicana Dome. Florida baseball fans were often northern transplants who retained their original team loyalties or retirees on fixed incomes. So even though the Marlins won World Series in 1997 and 2003, and the Rays were a consistent contender with a World Series appearance in 2008, both franchises remain troubled by low attendance.

The Colorado Rockies' emergence as an NL expansion team in 1993 became a throwback to the oddball stadium issues of earlier start-up franchises. Original home Mile High Stadium, home of the Denver Broncos, and successor Coors Field became baseball's version of a pinball game with frequent football-sized scores in the 5,000-foot altitude. Baseballs were stored in a humidor in an attempt to tone them down. The annual pitching problems have limited the Rockies' success, but they still made the wild card playoff in 1995 and the World Series in 2007.

Meanwhile, the Arizona Diamondbacks, the last expansion franchise in the NL in 1998, peaked early and have struggled to regain their initial success. Aggressive spending on talent resulted in a contender in 1999 and a dramatic championship in the 9/11-delayed World Series in 2001, but burdened the franchise with due bills in ensuing years. Only two of the 14 expansion teams—the Expos, now reborn as the Washington Nationals, and the Mariners—had not reached a World Series through 2015.

Domed Stadiums
Baseball Played in Inhospitable Climes

Baseball could never have been played in Houston and Phoenix without domed stadiums to ward off some of the most torrid temperatures experienced in the continental United States. Nor could it have stuck around without the assurance of indoor competition in small-market Milwaukee, where fans' wariness to watch games in cold, inclement weather made the Brewers a shaky proposition in the early- and mid-1990s.

The Astrodome in Houston was so sensational when unveiled in 1965 that it was called the "Eighth Wonder of the World." In southeast Texas there was air-conditioned comfort and space-age bells and whistles.

Today the Astros, as well as the Seattle Mariners, are housed in a second-generation dome, the retractable kind. Covered stadiums—never the cure-alls their original builders believed them to be—are no longer novelties. One team, the Minnesota Twins, has even done a 180-degree turn from dwelling in an ugly but effective dome in which they won two World Series to a sparkling outdoor stadium exposed to the chill of spring and (potentially) late autumn.

The bottom line is that the baseball landscape would look dramatically different if domed stadiums did not exist. Toronto, Tampa/St. Petersburg, and Miami joined the above-mentioned teams in performing under a roof. Indoor baseball always goes back to the Astrodome, but domed stadiums had been talked about for a decade prior to Houston's innovation, particularly when Dodgers owner Walter O'Malley first went fishing for a new ballpark in Brooklyn to replace Ebbets Field. But it took the vision of the colorful Judge Roy Hofheinz, the founding Astros owner, to bring the concept to fruition.

An aerial shot of the Astrodome with Houston, Texas, in the background

Houston could not have been awarded one of the two National League expansion franchises without the assurance of a domed ballpark. Although the Buffs were a legendary Triple-A franchise, major-league playing and spectating standards could not have been met in the sultry summer climate of Houston. Fans endured hardships in the heat at Hofheinz's temporary ballpark, Colt Stadium, named after the original Colt .45 team name, while the Astrodome was being built. When the Astrodome finally opened, Hofheinz reveled in the hoopla. The Yankees came to Houston for the first exhibition game, and Mickey Mantle homered as if to christen the ballpark. Everything was Texas-sized: a huge animated scoreboard, new for a stodgy game, exhorted fans when to clap; suites, also new, entertained the Lone Star high rollers; big outfield dimensions and a dark hitting backdrop made the Astrodome a pitchers' ballpark.

The second domed stadium, Olympic Stadium, had been originally constructed for the 1976 Summer Games in Montreal, and was made available to the National League's Expos the next year. The stadium was fitted with a first-generation retractable dome that never worked properly. Meant to be shut only in the early-season chill and during rainstorms, the dome had to be kept closed. Olympic Stadium turned into a dank, dreary backdrop for baseball in an otherwise tourist-friendly bilingual metropolis that visiting players loved. Soon the stadium picked up the nickname "The Mausoleum." Between diminishing crowds and corporate support fleeing to Toronto due to the Quebec separatist movement, the Expos began losing air as a franchise, and eventually were taken over by Major League Baseball in a move to Washington, DC.

Baseball had far better luck with its second Canadian dome. The 1977 expansion Toronto Blue Jays played in Exhibition Stadium before moving into the spanking-new Skydome in 1989. The stadium's motorized retractable roof worked without a hitch. With a decent ballpark

On the Space-Age Dome

"It reminds me of what I imagine my first ride would be like in a flying saucer." —*Mickey Mantle, April 9, 1965, the day he hit the first home run in the Astrodome*

SPITBALLING

and an attached hotel to glamorize the package, the Jays made a dent in the NHL Maple Leafs–dominated market, thanks to back-to-back World Series victories in 1992 and 1993.

A dome welcomed the return of baseball to Seattle in 1977. The Kingdome assured games would be played amid the frequent rainy days of the Pacific Northwest. The closed confines proved a home-field advantage when the Mariners finally developed into a contender in 1995. But the stadium quickly became dated. Fortunately, the franchise was able to lead the building of Safeco Field, which is the only "open-air" dome in baseball. Even though a retractable roof covers the field in the event of rain, openings in the outfield wall prevent claustrophobia.

On the other end of the spectrum of close confines domes is Tropicana Field in St. Petersburg. The presence of that dome—already constructed in the 1980s—was the main selling point for local baseball boosters to try to lure teams like the White Sox and Giants. Finally, the area was awarded an AL expansion team in the Rays in 1998. The dome was rated one of the worst stadiums in the country and fans responded accordingly. Despite a series of contenders and a World Series entrant under the former team of manager Joe Maddon and GM Andrew Friedman, the Rays are among the tail-enders in baseball attendance.

Meanwhile, the assurance of playing every game no matter the weather has saved baseball for Milwaukee. Then-owner Bud Selig had to do handsprings to get state legislative approval to build Miller Park. Brewers fans began staying away in droves from creaky, cramped open-air County Stadium after the team's peak seasons in the 1980s. Bad weather gave them a prime excuse. Locals said Brewers fans in central Wisconsin preferred to drive to the Twin Cities for the relative climate-control of the Metrodome than tailgate and spectate under less than ideal conditions at County Stadium. But once Miller Park flung open its gates and the team began contending again, the Brewers began drawing more than three million fans.

The assurance of playing every game no matter the weather has saved baseball for Milwaukee.

The reverse took place in the Twin Cities. While the good people of the Upper Midwest never had to worry about a rainout—or snowout—in the ugly Metrodome, they pined for outdoor baseball. After all, the Twins have Minnesota's 10,000 lakes as outdoor summer competition. Target Field became a reality in 2009, ending the crazy bounces on the Metrodome's funky artificial turf, weather-related mishaps with the roof—and the comeback World Series victories in 1987 and 1991.

An indoor stadium was a must in Phoenix before Major League Baseball could even award the desert metropolis an expansion franchise in the mid-1990s. BankOne Ballpark, later renamed Chase Field, keeps fans comfortable enough with the roof closed.

Artificial Turf

Neither Good Enough for Horses nor Ballplayers

"If a horse can't eat it, I don't want to play on it."

So said Dick Allen, whose moon shots needed no help from groundcover.

Artificial turf (commonly known as AstroTurf) seemed of great benefit at the time of its birth. It was modern, efficient. Entering the baseball with the multipurpose, cookie-cutter stadiums that proliferated in the early 1970s, faux grass allowed games to be played inside domed stadiums and permitted, say, football teams to use facilities without chewing up the field.

In the long run, though, what got chewed up were athletes' knees and other body parts enduring stress on the hard surfaces, which were not perfected by any means in their first generation. And if a player's joints held up, he often got a literal hot-foot with the artificial turf heating up to 130 degrees on summer afternoons.

NO. 26

"I think AstroTurf had a huge impact on the game . . . ," said Hal Morris, former Cincinnati Reds first baseman and the Los Angeles Angels' pro scouting director as of 2015. "For several reasons, it definitely affected the players on the field. It is a harder surface than natural grass [especially older turf], and was much more demanding on a player's body.

"Due to its hardness, it impacted one's knees, lower back and hamstrings. I had issues with all three of these areas during my playing career, and I have no doubt that these were in part caused by the turf."

The turf was first installed by necessity when the original grass field at Houston's Astrodome died out in 1965 for lack of exposure to direct sunlight.

Speedy center fielder Willie Wilson was one of the Royals players who thrived on artificial turf in the 1980s.

A new kind of turf called ChemGrass had been under development by Monsanto for several years when Judge Roy Hofheinz, the Astros' owner and builder of the Astrodome, realized he needed a replacement for '65's failed natural surface. It was rebranded AstroTurf in coordination with its new indoor home and the team's name.

The Chicago White Sox installed the first artificial surface at an outdoor ballpark. Old Comiskey Park's infield and adjoining foul territory were carpeted for the 1969 season, while the outfield remained grass. The arrangement lasted until Bill Veeck acquired the Sox for the second time for the 1976 season.

The 1970 season was the big leap forward for artificial surfaces. St. Louis's Busch Stadium installed the turf. Cincinnati's Riverfront Stadium and Pittsburgh's Three Rivers Stadium opened at mid-season with AstroTurf, fully ready to double up in hosting the NFL's Bengals and Steelers, respectively. Philadelphia's Veterans Stadium then came turf-equipped when it flung open its multipurpose doors for the Phillies in 1971.

The baseball-only Kauffman Stadium in Kansas City was built in 1973 with new turf. Meanwhile, the succession of domed stadiums that followed the Astrodome—Olympic Stadium in Montreal, the Kingdome in Seattle, the Metrodome in Minneapolis, the Skydome with its retractable roof in Toronto, and Tropicana Field in St. Petersburg—all used artificial turf.

By the mid-1970s, the artificial surfaces had a track record of poor reviews due to the strange bounces of the baseballs and, above all, the stress on the players themselves. Having the worst time of it was future Hall of Famer Andre Dawson, who came into pro baseball with

On the Bouncing Ball

"Artificial turf did indeed intimidate teams that did not play on it at home. On July 2, 1977, before 50,534 at Busch Stadium II, the Cubs committed five errors in the first inning, leading to four Cardinals runs, in a 10–3 loss. The ball was bouncing high and every which way off the hard turf, almost mesmerizing the jittery Cubs. Pitcher Bill Bonham and normally sure-handed second baseman Manny Trillo each committed two miscues, while left fielder Gene Clines had one." —*author George Castle's personal remembrance*

SPITBALLING

the lingering effects of high school knee surgery. Dawson played 10 seasons on the Montreal turf, then campaigned to play on the Wrigley Field grass. He signed a blank contract, later filled in for $500,000, to make the switch during the year of owners' collusion. "I wouldn't have played 20 years if I had not gotten off the AstroTurf," said Dawson.

Morris reported negative effects for himself and visiting players on the Riverfront Stadium turf. "I believe that I would have played more games during my career and had fewer DL stints had I played on a grass surface the entire time," he said. "As an example of the effect it had on players' bodies, I can remember that Robbie Thompson and Will Clark would typically not play an entire series when they came to Cincinnati with the Giants."

Players learned to be creative in trying to cool and cushion their feet when temperatures soared to far above 100 degrees on the turf. "You can't really protect your shoes," said Dawson. "Your feet got warm. I learned how to play with turf shoes because running on the turf with spikes, you sort of dug into it and there wasn't a lot of give to it and it made it that much harder. The rubber shoes gave you more of a cushion. I used spikes to dig in at the batter's box. You got on base, you want to change into different shoes. I learned how to play in rubber shoes all the time."

On defense, the infielders had to be wary of high hops. In the outfield, Gold Glove players like Dawson learned how to allow for extra bounces depending on how the ball came off the bat. All players had to worry about the ball making contact with any exposed seams.

All players had to worry about the ball making contact with any exposed seams.

"Montreal had a few areas where seams were kind of exposed," Dawson said. "It was more of a hindrance. The ball could hit a seam and be misdirected. It was bouncy when it was hot. When it was wet, it was different. It didn't bounce as much, but it skidded."

Artificial turf proliferated at football stadiums across the country, too. But the mania began to wane in the 1990s as a building boom began for spanking-new baseball parks with retro features and natural surfaces. Catastrophic injuries took place on the turf, further hastening its removal. On October 13, 1993, Chicago Bears wide receiver Wendell Davis severed both patella tendons after being driven back to the turf in a game against the Eagles at Veterans Stadium. Davis had planted his feet to snare a pass, but they got stuck in the turf. His kneecaps were pushed into his thighs. He never played another down in the NFL.

Softer, higher-tech versions of artificial turf have been developed going into the new millennium. But baseball isn't buying. New retractable domed stadiums have installed grass, which is cultivated with the roof open during the day well before gametimes.

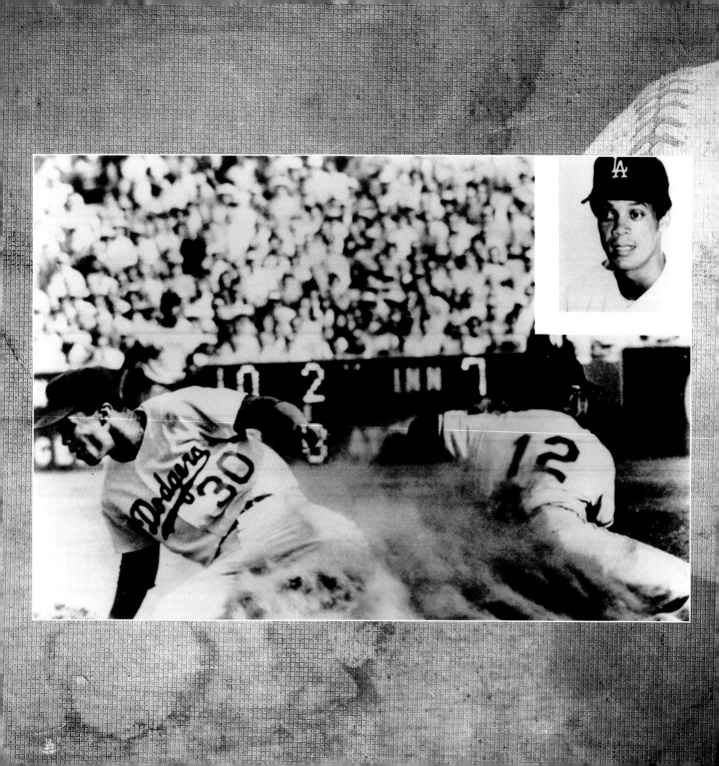

Maury Wills and the Stolen Base

"Go, Maury, Go!" and Baseball Has Never Stopped Running

NO.

27

Slender and eager, Maury Wills ran the game into a new era with his startling 104 stolen bases to open Dodger Stadium in 1962. Another 12 years transpired before Wills's main competitor, Lou Brock, surpassed that record. And still a new decade would begin before multiple players exceeded 100 steals, with Rickey Henderson establishing himself as the best leadoff man of all time, locking down the all-time season high of 130 thefts. And, despite the misconception that the PEDs-inflated power era of the 1990s slowed the sprinting, baseball has never fully returned to its laggard pace in stealing bases.

The game will never regress to the pre-Wills, heavy-legged, baggy-pantsed days. Low-gear feats included Stan Hack of the Cubs leading the National League in steals with just 16 in 1938 and 17 in 1939. Future two-time world-champion Pirates manager Danny Murtaugh paced the senior circuit with 18 in 1941 and the Red Sox's Dom DiMaggio established a league-leading modern-day low with an AL-best 15 in 1950.

In baseball's ancient history, and stretching several decades into the modern era after 1900, the stolen base actually was a crucial tactic. "Sliding Billy" Hamilton amassed four seasons of 100 or more steals and one with 97 between 1889 and 1895. The irascible Ty Cobb

Maury Wills arrives at his preferred destination on the basepaths amid a cloud of dust. Wills was the first major leaguer to steal at least 100 bases.

then took over to supplement his sublime hitting with dominant legs to set the modern-day record of 96 steals in 1915, to go along with season totals of 83, 76, and 68.

But as with other crucial aspects of baseball, the 1920 season became the demarcation line. Transforming to a power-oriented game thanks to Babe Ruth, baseball slowed to a crawl when someone led off first base. One wouldn't want to hinder a sluggers' ability to belt the pelota over the fences. The prevailing orthodoxy was best expressed by former Cubs "head coach" Bob Kennedy: He admitted that he ill-advisedly failed to let the quicksilver Brock run more aggressively in 1963 because he did not want to take the bats out of the hands of Billy Williams and Ron Santo.

Jackie Robinson gained renown with daring baserunning that threw opponents into a defensive tizzy as he broke the color line in 1947. But Robinson led the NL with only 29 steals in 1947, yielding the thievery crown to rookie Phillies outfielder Richie Ashburn with 32 in 1948, then reclaiming the prize with 37 steals in his 1949 MVP season.

More typical of the times were the 25 thefts each by Billy Bruton of the Milwaukee Braves and Jim Rivera of the White Sox to lead their respective leagues in 1955. Opportunity created the proto-Wills in 1959. Teaming with No. 2 hitter and AL MVP Nellie Fox, White Sox leadoff man "Little Looie" Aparicio turned on the jets to steal 56 for a pennant-winning team severely short on power. Comiskey Park fans chanted "Go! Go! Go!" when Aparicio led off first. But Wills was supremely motivated to run and would never stop until age overtook him. He made his big-league debut at 26 for the Dodgers in 1959. Replacing Jim Gilliam as the Dodgers' leadoff hitter in the second half of the 1960 season, Wills was finally able to run freely. He stole 50 bases, the first National Leaguer since Max Carey in 1923 to reach that total. Urged

On the Players Protecting Ty Cobb's Stolen Base Record

"[Larry] Jackson threw over to first 16 times. Bill White was the first baseman and every time I went diving back into first base, he'd slap the ball down hard on my head or face. They were killing me." —*Maury Wills to* Los Angeles Times *columnist Bill Dwyre in 2012*

SPITBALLING

on by Dodger Stadium crowds chanting, "Go! Go! Go, Maury, Go!," Wills set up an uncommonly robust Dodgers lineup in 1962. Tommy Davis drove in 153 runs while Frank Howard blasted 31 homers in the spacious new ballpark. His 208 hits, including an NL-leading 10 triples, set up his theft spree. But while paying a heavy physical toll, Wills never got roughed up more than when he sought to break Cobb's record against Larry Jackson of the Cardinals in St. Louis in Game No. 156. Jackson threw over to first a grueling 16 times.

Wills's compensation was the NL's 1962 MVP award.

Wills's style was not immediately copied through most of baseball. But Cardinals manager Johnny Keane had paid attention. After a Cardinals September surge was finally stymied by the Dodgers in 1963, Keane wanted his own Wills. He got him the next season in Brock and what turned out to be the best trade in Cardinals history. Hitting .348 with 33 steals the last two-thirds of the 1964 season, Brock's transformation propelled St. Louis to a World Series victory.

Wills stole 94 bases to goose an offensively challenged (and Sandy Koufax–centered) Dodgers team to the championship in 1965, but soon was surpassed by Brock. The Cardinals' speedster swiped between 51 and 70 bases each season from 1967 to 1973. Brock, then 35, exceeded his own standards to break Wills's record with 118 steals in 1974. With Henderson following Wills's blazing trail, the golden age of thievery commenced.

Henderson broke in with the Athletics in 1979, opened the 1980s with 100 steals, and then locked in the all-time record with 130 thefts in 1982. Henderson's encore was 108 thefts in 1983. Moving cross-country to the Yankees, Henderson racked up 80, 87, and 93 steals through 1988. Back with the Athletics in 1990, Henderson complemented his 65 steals with 28 homers and a .439 on-base percentage. When his amazing 25-year career concluded, Henderson had a record 1,406 steals.

No enterprising thief has come close to 100 steals since the '80s heyday.

Vince Coleman rounded up a lightning-fast Cardinals "Whiteyball" (for manager Whitey Herzog) lineup on Busch Stadium's artificial turf with three straight seasons of 110, 107, and 109 steals from 1985 to 1987. Meanwhile, in the mausoleum atmosphere of Montreal's Olympic Stadium, Tim Raines totaled 70 or more steals each season from 1981 to 1986. In the final two seasons in that period, Raines stole 70 each and was caught just nine times each.

No enterprising thief has come close to 100 steals since the '80s heyday. The 2014 and '15 postseason success of the Kansas City Royals promised to stoke the concept that swift players could make a lot out of a comparative little. But long before the Royals' entertaining run, Wills proved that speed, properly utilized, never takes a day off.

The June Amateur Draft

Giving Lesser Teams a Chance to Rise Again

Is the June amateur draft an inexact science? Let's look at the eventual big leaguers drafted in the first and second rounds in 1965 before the Cincinnati Reds picked catcher Johnny Bench out of Binger High School in rural Oklahoma.

Powerful left-handed-hitting Arizona State outfielder Rick Monday was the first pick of that first-ever draft. Monday slugged a memorable Dodgers playoff homer in 1981, and slugged 241 homers over parts of 19 seasons. OK, good player, and also a good guy still holding forth in the Dodgers' broadcast booth.

Next up was Les Rohr, a bit-part Met. Then Joe Coleman, who won 62 games for the Tigers from 1971 to 1973. Billy Conigliaro complemented his more famous slugging brother Tony. Rick James was a cup-of-coffee-Cub. Ray Fosse got run over by Pete Rose to end the 1970 All-Star Game before joining Monday as a broadcast mainstay. Eddie Leon was a proverbial peppery middle infielder. Jim Spencer slugged 146 homers as a platoon first baseman for five teams. Gene Lamont had a much longer life as a manager and coach than as a backup catcher. Third baseman Al Gallagher was renowned for his nickname "Dirty Al." Bernie Carbo, the Reds' first pick, was better known for a pinch-hit homer against his old team in the 1975 World Series.

Mike Adamson and Bill Burbach rounded out the first-round picks who got promoted to "The Show." Further up in the the second round were Joe Keough, Keith Lampard, Ken Rudolph, Alan Foster, Del Unser, and Sandy Vance. Finally—with the 16th pick of the

Johnny Bench thought he'd be a Cub, but Chicago's passing on him twice in the inaugural 1965 amateur draft enabled the Reds to select him.

second round—the Reds got around to selecting Bench, who had expected to be drafted by the Cubs.

Bill Capps, the Cubs' area scout based out of Dallas, pleaded with the front office to pick Bench. But high school pitcher James and college outfielder-catcher Rudolph, eventually no better than a backup catcher in the majors, somehow gained the Wrigley Field bosses' loyalty over a kid catcher who could have succeeded the likes of Ed Bailey, Chris Krug, and Vic Roznovsky in a couple of years. But, hey, the Reds took hard-hitting outfielder Carbo over Bench. The sequence proves the old adage of it's not how you start, it's how you finish—and Bench ended up in Cooperstown as perhaps the best-ever catcher.

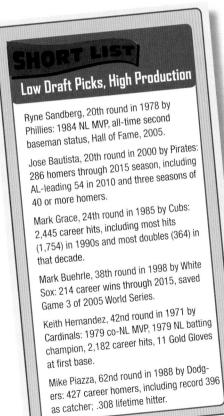

SHORT LIST

Low Draft Picks, High Production

Ryne Sandberg, 20th round in 1978 by Phillies: 1984 NL MVP, all-time second baseman status, Hall of Fame, 2005.

Jose Bautista, 20th round in 2000 by Pirates: 286 homers through 2015 season, including AL-leading 54 in 2010 and three seasons of 40 or more homers.

Mark Grace, 24th round in 1985 by Cubs: 2,445 career hits, including most hits (1,754) in 1990s and most doubles (364) in that decade.

Mark Buehrle, 38th round in 1998 by White Sox: 214 career wins through 2015, saved Game 3 of 2005 World Series.

Keith Hernandez, 42nd round in 1971 by Cardinals: 1979 co-NL MVP, 1979 NL batting champion, 2,182 career hits, 11 Gold Gloves at first base.

Mike Piazza, 62nd round in 1988 by Dodgers: 427 career homers, including record 396 as catcher; .308 lifetime hitter.

The draft, like other facets of slow-reacting baseball instituted decades after the NFL and NBA versions, put an end to an inequitable system where wealthier teams still landed the best amateur talent in an era when signing bonuses were more limited. A rule, in effect the majority of seasons between 1947 and 1965, forced teams who signed an amateur for more than $4,000 to keep that player on the parent club for his first two seasons. Only then could he be optioned to the minors. Later, the big-league break-in requirement was dropped to one year for these "bonus babies." Amazingly, four Hall of Famers came out of this postwar system: Sandy Koufax, Harmon Killebrew, Al Kaline, and Catfish Hunter. Of the quartet, only Killebrew spent any time in the minor leagues.

It was every man for himself in the scouting game, and who would succeed depended upon a scout's savvy and persuasiveness combined with the prospect's interest in the bidding clubs. In his Cubs scouting days, Hall of Fame–bound Buck O'Neil used his silver tongue to sign African-American prospects, assuring them they had a quicker path to the majors with the stumblebum parent club than through Dodgers or Giants organizations loaded with talent. But in the bonus baby years, O'Neil and his embattled colleagues had less money to work with than opponents. Talented West Coast Cubs colleague Gene Handley offered Los Angeles prep pitching whiz Larry Dierker $35,000 to sign in 1964. But Paul Richards of the expansion Colt .45s blew out the established franchise offer with $50,000 to land Dierker, who as an 18-year-old was in Houston's starting rotation in 1965.

At the same time Richards shelled out for Dierker, a huge bidding war commenced for University of Wisconsin two-sports star Rick Reichardt. A veteran of the 1963 Rose Bowl squad at fullback, Reichardt was even more highly rated in baseball. The Los Angeles Angels won out with a $200,000 signing bonus, twice the highest salary of a big-league star of the time. Reserve-clause era owners finally instituted cost controls with a draft.

In theory the draft was a game changer, enabling poorest-finishing clubs to get the best talent by picking first. But Bench's entry into pro baseball and eventual superstar status exemplifies the crapshoot of the draft.

Roughly half of the draft's number one picks never make it. Another player slipping further down will end up as a superstar. Far less certainty exists for a drafted player than his counterparts in the NFL and NBA, who usually build up to their top-rated status at a big-name college program. A baseball player coming out of high school is a tough projection.

Roughly half of the draft's number one picks never make it.

In an era when every player's feats are chronicled and streamed on the Internet, a talented hitting prospect is less likely to slip all the way through the draft. Scouting guru Tim Wilken once said teams must corral talented hitting prospects in the high rounds or risk losing out. The next 10 drafts after 1965 proved that the key to an organization's success was the depth of its picks. Teams could not count on the number one pick in the entire draft as a savior.

Despite some spectacular failures, the system did work in the long run. Teams that dropped to bottom-feeder status for years eventually rose up again through the draft—provided they had dynamic management that knew how to scout and develop. But the biggest feat might have been achieved by the Atlanta Braves to keep their supremacy atop the National League East going. Drafting last or near to last thanks to constant first-place divisional finishes from 1991 through the mid-2000s, the Braves kept the talent flow going through their disciplined player development system, slipping only in the 2010s.

And if baseball was tardy compared to other sports with instituting a draft, the grand ol' game was better late than never in televising and hyping the draft in the 2010s. The event was bound to move up in stature with online exposure. An imprecise process, the draft nevertheless became a less glamorous game changer over the past half-century.

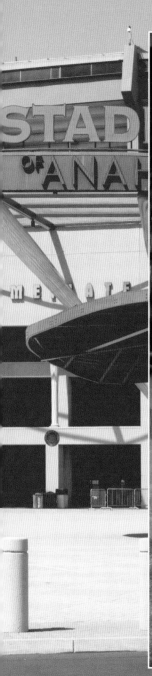

Night World Series Games

Altering a Traditional October Institution

The youthful World Series fan from 1963 was used to smuggling a transistor radio and earphone into class to surreptitiously follow the play-by-play on the local NBC-Radio affiliate. Or, if he were lucky, he'd have an indulgent teacher who'd wheel the school's sole television set into the class to watch two national heroes, Sandy Koufax and Mickey Mantle, duel each other.

Thrust the lad six decades into the future to watch the Fall Classic, and he'd be totally disoriented.

Instead of a weekday 1:00 p.m. EST game ending in time for the *Match Game* hosted by Gene Rayburn in the East and Midwest, and maybe a *Bachelor Father* rerun on the West Coast, he'd fight encroaching sleep from bleary eyes amid a ninth inning. Why so late? The first pitch took place around 8:30 p.m., delaying the late news until midnight—or later. The creeping afternoon fall shadows making Koufax super-unhittable in the ninth inning are now mediocre visibility for the first few innings of a game from the West Coast. The presence of Indian summer—it was in the 80s and even 90s in much of the country in early October 1963—would be traded for hints of winter and trick or treat stragglers on Halloween night.

Furthermore, the kid would punch the remote on a weekend midday to find nothing but college football on Saturdays and the NFL on Sundays. The World Series dare not compete head-to-head against the gridiron colossuses and consigns itself to timeslots formerly reserved for *Lawrence Welk* on Saturday nights and *Bonanza* on Sunday evenings.

Thwarted years before in daytime postseason flops, the Angels let loose under the lights celebrating their first World Series title in 2002.

The World Series was once a shared national experience—for those who were fortunate to get within earshot of a radio at work or school, or the smaller numbers within eyesight of a TV set during the 9-to-5 grind. Decisions on placement of baseball programming that began in the mid-1960s sought to rectify the fans' dilemma of not easily being able to watch.

It worked, initially, with dramatically increased ratings for primetime World Series games that began in 1971. But over the decades one set of problems replaced another as the uniqueness of the World Series, once the only game in town in its timeslot, has dramatically diminished. The "jewel event" now intrudes not only into the halfway point of the football season, but also well into the regular season of the NBA and NHL.

After their comeback World Series triumph against the Giants in 2002, the Angels pile up and begin a night of partying.

First hints of change from day to night came with a huge increase in TV money. NBC paid $11.8 million a year from 1965 to 1967 for the Saturday Game of the Week, the World Series, and the All-Star Game. To recoup some of those costs, NBC first got Major League Baseball to agree to primetime telecasts on national holidays, then the first night All-Star Game from the new Angels' stadium in Anaheim in 1967.

Despite the primetime All-Star and holiday games, the World Series remained pristine as a daytime-only attraction until after the NFL achieved a tipping point for nighttime sports. ABC-TV's signature *Monday Night Football* series began in 1970 and was an immediate hit. Finally, on Wednesday, October 13, 1971, in Pittsburgh, baseball staged its first primetime World Series game. More than 60 million watched. The viewership steadily grew throughout the years and indelible moments. On October 27, 1986, a night after Mookie Wilson's grounder snaked through Bill Buckner's legs, the viewership grew to 81 million for Game 7 of the classic New York Mets–Boston Red Sox showdown.

But the audience's choices were much narrower than in a later millennium. Even in the 1980s, cable penetration had not yet matured in much of the country, particularly some big cities. The three-channel, three-network universe still held sway. A World Series, such as in 1978, could draw a 50 percent share (percentage of total TV households).

Major League Baseball instituted its League Championship Series in 1969. But it was still only best-of-five, pushing the World Series back just one week. The most memorable postseason moments still were reserved for the Fall Classic (see 1975 and 1986). Daytime World Series games were moved to primetime by the late 1980s.

Then, in 1995 in the wake of the disastrous strike, Major League Baseball instituted the best-of-five Division Series to accommodate a wild card entrant as the start of the postseason. Suddenly, the abject drama of the World Series was diluted with even more playoff drama.

Pushed back even more, the World Series began its creep to the very end of October. 9/11, which interrupted baseball for a week, prompted the World Series to begin on October 27, with Game 5 in Yankee Stadium on November 1, the first-ever Fall Classic game in that month. The Yankees-Diamondbacks affair was concluded with a dramatic ninth-inning rally by the D'Backs on November 4 in Phoenix.

9/11, which interrupted baseball for a week, prompted the World Series to begin on October 27, with Game 5 in Yankee Stadium on November 1, the first-ever Fall Classic game in that month.

Autumn weather in northern climes finally bit baseball in its sensitive spot on Monday, October 27, 2008, in Philadelphia. A steady rain had made the field all but unplayable when umpires called a halt to Game 5 of the Rays-Phillies contest in the top of the sixth inning. Another day of rain on October 28 postponed the resumption to the next night.

The Halloween border was trampled upon in 2009 and 2010. The Yankees-Phillies World Series did not begin until October 28, concluding November 4 at Yankee Stadium. In 2010, the Giants and Texas Rangers began October 27 and concluded November 1 in Arlington, Texas.

All the while the World Series slipped toward November, it received competition from hundreds of new sources compared to the mid-1980s. The Fox Network, which snared a share of the baseball package, preceded several other new programming chains in offering national primetime entertainment choices. ESPN was first among equals on a hundreds-of-channels cable universe, offering first-rate primetime sports programming. Regional cable sports networks sprung up in most pro markets. Both subscription and online services now give consumers almost too many choices in video entertainment.

Viewership has declined into the 12- to 15-million range. Game 7s, such as those in 2011 and 2014, seem to be the only way to goose the numbers to 23 to 25 million.

Curt Flood
Baseball's Ultimate Team Player

In baseball parlance, Curt Flood gave himself up both on and off the field.

Capable of hitting at batting-champ levels with a .335 seasonal career best, Flood likely left some hits on the table at mid-career when he was the lineup man protecting Lou Brock's base-stealing, so crucial to three St. Louis Cardinals' pennants and two World Series titles between 1964 and 1968.

Off the field, Flood made the ultimate sacrifice, challenging the reserve clause in a manner no other player had done. Metaphorically, he worked the count, wearing down the proverbial opposition, moving the runner along, putting hidebound baseball tradition—binding a player forever to the team that held his contract—squarely in the spotlight of a society open to change.

NO. 30

As a skilled hitter who fashioned defensive skills in center as sublime as those of Willie Mays, Flood knew timing was everything. And in his case, his challenge to the reserve clause, which went all the way to the Supreme Court, might not have even occurred had he been traded a year or two later from his longtime base in St. Louis. As part of Players Association guru Marvin Miller's steady gathering of players' rights prior to free agency, the collective bargaining agreement of 1970 provided that 10-year-veteran players who had been with the same team for the previous five seasons could veto a trade. Flood qualified on both counts with the Cardinals. He could have blocked the deal if the timing was different. But it wasn't, and his life—and that of baseball—moved in a radically different direction.

Over the decades, Flood's selflessness in essentially trashing a career with at least several productive seasons and perhaps $400,000 in earnings (in 1970s dollars) remaining hasn't been fully appreciated by the players enjoying the full bloom of free-agent rights. Fortunately, three years before his premature death at 59 from throat cancer in 1997, the

Curt Flood as a prosperous Cardinals center fielder in the late 1960s.
Flood already had been a civil rights activist by this point.

players preparing to strike got a pep talk from Flood. He had a good baseball life as the 60s drew to a close. Earning $90,000, one of baseball's top salaries, he had put down roots in the community with outside business interests, including portrait painting that got nationwide publicity. His portrait of Cardinals owner Gussie Busch hung front and center in the bar of the Budweiser baron's yacht. But Busch got increasingly restive as Miller clamored for workplace rights and a fairer share of baseball's revenue stream. Busch gave a "where is your loyalty"–style lecture to the Cardinals with reporters watching near the end of spring training in 1969. After that season, with the Redbirds slumping to fourth place in the new National League East, Busch mandated a housecleaning. Flood was summarily dispatched to Philadelphia in a multi-player deal that netted slugger Dick Allen in return.

Flood knew full well what being traded to Philly meant. He would go from a close-knit, racially harmonious team that had been in contention almost straight through since 1963 to a 99-loss franchise that had a deserved reputation for poor race relations. The Phillies had been the last National League team to integrate in 1957. Flood wrote that Philadelphia was "the nation's northernmost southern city."

But even more motivating than being forced to leave was principle. "I want to sue baseball on constitutional grounds," he told Miller in their first post-trade meeting. "I want to give the courts a chance to outlaw the reserve system. I want to go out like a man instead of disappearing like a bottle cap."

Busch and Devine had picked the wrong man to go quietly. Flood had long been a civil rights activist, unlike the majority of black players of his era, mindful of their place in a conservative game that did not even allow facial hair until 1972. He had lobbied for desegregation of the

On the Reserve System

"I do not feel that I am a piece of property to be bought and sold irrespective of my wishes."
—*Curt Flood in a letter to Commissioner Bowie Kuhn*

SPITBALLING

Cardinals' spring training living quarters at the dawn of the 60s. In 1962, Jackie Robinson invited Flood to speak at a regional NAACP convention in Jackson, Mississippi, earning Flood a file with the racist Mississippi State Sovereignty Commission. He fought to rent a home in a white neighborhood near his Oakland, California, hometown in the fall of 1964, winning the battle and earning support of neighbors and local law enforcement officials.

Some folks pegged Flood as an anarchist trying to gut baseball. But like Miller, he simply wanted the system to be modified through collective bargaining. Interestingly, that was the same recommendation arbitrator Peter Seitz, who opened the floodgates to free agency in 1975, had repeatedly relayed to the owners. "After the courts rule that the present reserve system is unlawful," Flood wrote hopefully in *The Way It Is*, "the employers will be obligated to do what they should have done years ago. They will sit down with the players and negotiate reasonable conditions of employment."

At the Supreme Court, the principle of stare decisis ("to stand by things decided") won out due to legal precedent protecting baseball's anti-trust exemptions.

Flood waged the good fight in the courts. Arguing on his behalf was Arthur Goldberg, former Supreme Court justice, US secretary of labor, and US ambassador to the United Nations. Robinson and fellow Hall of Famer Hank Greenberg testified on his behalf.

At the Supreme Court, the principle of *stare decisis* ("to stand by things decided") won out due to legal precedent protecting baseball's anti-trust exemptions. The high court ruled 5–3 against Flood's suit, with Justice Lewis Powell recusing himself because of ownership in stock of Anheuser-Busch, which owned Flood's former team. Justice Harry Blackmun admitted baseball was a business that engaged in interstate commerce, theoretically putting it under the anti-trust microscope. But Blackman also rationalized the game was "an exception and an anomaly" and an "established aberration." The court thus upheld tradition in an era when it consistently advanced the cause of civil and personal rights. As Miller essentially predicted, Flood's big-league career was over. He'd work one year as an Athletics broadcaster in 1978 and dabbled in an upstart baseball league a decade later. Flood's sacrifice was recognized late in life, and posthumously. A creative thinker, he knew being on the right side of history wouldn't necessarily be recognized immediately. Flood addressed the players just before they went out on the devastating strike in 1994. Eighteen years after his death, in 2015, both the Hall of Fame and Players Association president Tony Clark paid tribute to Flood during the annual Awards Presentation one day before the induction ceremonies in Cooperstown.

Someone had to be first to say what was wrong had to be made right.

Arbitration
If Owners Hate It, They Have Only Themselves to Blame

NO.31

In the years before the reserve clause was gutted by arbitrator Peter Seitz, owners, chief negotiator John Gaherin, and commissioner Bowie Kuhn favored arbitration as a means to end salary holdouts and beat the players at salary disputes. Gaherin also believed, for strategic reasons, that arbitration could be used to forestall the eventual assault on the reserve clause. In the long run, however, the system boosted paychecks and forced owners to sign players to contracts close to their preferred levels to avoid losing an arbitration case. Numerous multi-year contracts given to players early in their careers also resulted from owners eager to keep budding stars out of the arbitration process. Arbitration had its roots in the first Basic Agreement in 1968, providing for a formal grievance procedure. Binding impartial arbitration to settle disputes came two years later. Finally, in 1973, the owners agreed to arbitration for players with two or more years' experience by an overwhelming 22–2 vote. Players no longer had to threaten offseason holdouts and then capitulate as Opening Day neared.

Nay-sayers in the vote were Athletics owner Charlie Finley, who treated his players like serfs, and the Cardinals, where owner Gussie Busch had grown increasingly cantankerous about player compensation.

"Give them anything they want, but don't give them arbitration," Finley warned as the first cases were heard in February 1974. The A's accounted for nine of the 29 inaugural hearings.

Busch actually had been generous by the game's pay standards for his World Series teams in the 1960s, but joined the old guard in resisting the inevitable changes in compensation and player rights in the new decade. He traded Steve Carlton to the Phillies in 1972 after being just $10,000 apart in respective salary demands. Carlton had the last word by notching

Bruce Sutter pitches in a Cardinals uniform. Sutter showed the dangers of a team not agreeing to a contract prior to arbitration.

27 victories for a team that won just 59 overall, punching his eventual ticket to the Hall of Fame. "Lefty"'s dispute was two years too soon for arbitration's benefits.

Players Association chief Marvin Miller saw arbitration as an important step in acquiring workplace rights common in other industries. As he wrote in his 1991 autography, *A Whole Different Ball Game: The Sport and Business of Baseball*: "The difference between a ballplayer's being required to accept whatever a club offered him, as had been the case almost since the beginning of professional baseball, and the new system of salary arbitration was like the difference between dictatorship and democracy. Salary arbitration has been a major factor in eliminating gross inequities in the salary structures from club to club (and sometimes on the same club)."

The inherent system caused far more conflict than free agency. A club submitted a figure, contrasting with the player's. The arbitrator was mandated to pick one or the other, based on each side's arguments. That meant a team trotted out negative information about their own player in an effort to achieve the lower number. But given the possibility of the player winning via a huge pay hike, the majority of arbitration filings ended up with the team settling with the player, most often with a nice raise.

Baseball executives further criticized the system as being handled by arbitrators who did not have an insider's knowledge of the game.

"I think the arbiters are non-baseball people who don't understand and don't have a feel for the true value of a ballplayer," said longtime honcho Dallas Green. "What you end up with is years of service making more and more decisions instead of performance. We've gotten away from paying for performance. . . . Arbitration to me is an agent's tool that does nothing but bad things for baseball." But facts were facts. Players enjoying great seasons presented powerful cases for arbitration. Finley railed against his own stars in his first set of arbitration cases in 1974. First, third baseman Sal Bando asked for $100,000, an increase from $75,000, and was granted his request. Then Finley fought against Reggie Jackson's desire to jump from $90,000 to $135,000 after leading the AL in homers, RBIs, and runs. Finley offered just $100,000. Again, the arbitrator ruled against Finley.

SHORT LIST

The Players versus A's Owner Charlie Finley in 1974, the First Year of Arbitration

Reggie Jackson—won
Sal Bando—won
Ken Holtzman—won
Rollie Fingers—won
Darold Knowles—won
Joe Rudi—lost
Gene Tenace—lost
Ted Kubiak—lost
Jack Heidemann—lost

But the colorful A's despot-owner didn't stop. When starter Ken Holtzman's and closer Rollie Fingers's cases were heard next, Finley tried to convince the arbitrator that Holtzman's 21-win season was due to Fingers's great relief work. In contrast, Finley claimed the Oakland rotation's fine work in holding down scoring was responsible for supposedly inflating Fingers's saves total.

"Finley did the jobs of four men—unfortunately, three of them were named Groucho, Chico and Harpo," mused Miller in his book. The lessons of Finley did not stick with his fellow magnates. Thrifty owners paid dearly for daring to go to arbitration, dramatically affecting the fortunes of multiple teams.

Thrifty owners paid dearly for daring to go to arbitration, dramatically affecting the fortunes of multiple teams.

After his 1979 Cy Young Award season, in which he was paid $225,000, Cubs split-fingered virtuoso closer Bruce Sutter and Cubs GM Bob Kennedy agreed on a five-year, $475,000-per-season contract. But Kennedy had to get owner Bill Wrigley's blessing for final approval. He didn't, as Wrigley refused to believe a player was worth nearly a half-million bucks per season. The third-generation gum magnate was under increasing financial pressure, soon buffeted by a $40 million inheritance-tax obligation that forced him to sell to Tribune Company in 1981.

Angered, Sutter invoked his arbitration rights, asking for the moon with $700,000. Agents Jim Bronner and Bob Gilhooley did not figure Sutter would get such a high award, but filed the stratospheric amount to create negotiating room with Kennedy. Wrigley cheaped out with a $350,000 arbitration number. The management presentation was conducted by future Cubs president Andy MacPhail, then a junior team executive. In an argument praised by both sides, the 27-year-old MacPhail argued that no third-year player ever had been paid $350,000—$20,000 more than established closer Goose Gossage.

Still, Sutter won the case. Wrigley ordered Kennedy to trade Sutter after the 1980 season. The deal to the Cardinals, as with the trade of Lou Brock back in 1964, helped St. Louis to a World Series victory in 1982 as Sutter recorded 36 saves. Meanwhile, Leon Durham, one of the players received from St. Louis, made a critical error at first base in Game 5 of the 1984 National League Championship Series as the Cubs coughed up a 2-games-to-0 lead against the Padres and once again were thwarted in their endless World Series quest.

The Sutter incident was a textbook warning for management to stay out of arbitration. The process is the ultimate sword of Damocles dangled over the owners' heads. Once again, they had miscalculated the tide of player rights as the 20th century proceeded.

PEDs

Only the Latest Way Players Have Tried to Beat a Game of Failure

Baseball is the ultimate game of failure. Its batting champions fail two out of three times at bat. A basketball player who makes just one of every three shots is on the bench or off the team. A quarterback cannot play if he completes just 33 percent of his passes.

A home-run and RBI champion in Triple-A may be typecast as a "Four-A" player if he quickly does not make it in the majors. Closers in particular operate on the razor's edge, the difference between a save and walk-off homer for the opponent being an inch's difference in pitch location.

NO. 32

With this athletic sword of Damocles hanging over their heads, players from the game's beginnings have sought means above and beyond their talent to fight off failure. Foreign substances have been applied to baseballs to make them dart away from bats. Field glasses were employed to steal catcher's signs from faraway center field perches (an original reason for baseball's lords to oppose the use of the center field camera in the 1950s). Corking bats was another low-tech method to aid performance, seen before, during, and after the PED era. Clubhouses came well stocked with amphetamines, popularly known as "greenies," for decades as a kind of super-caffeine to boost energy levels through the long season until they were recently banned.

If there is a way to circumvent rules and boost the output of well-sculpted, but often tired and injured bodies, players will find them, "perfect" them, and go to great lengths to conceal them.

PEDs were the most advanced, chemically based anti-failure devices available to players. In a way, their use likely starting in the 1980s was surprisingly late considering the allure elsewhere of body boosters.

The spectacular home-run race between Mark McGwire and Sammy Sosa in 1998 represented the peak of artificial stimulants uses.

"Look at the international athletes in the 70s," pointed out Dr. Charles Bush-Joseph, professor of orthopedic surgery and associate director of the Rush Orthopedic Sports Medicine Fellowship in Chicago. "There were always comments about the Soviet Union and the East German women. It really became evident to the average everyday [US] athlete that there's something they do that's different than what we do. Why do they grow their athletes bigger and stronger and have greater performance levels than we do?

"Yeah, the information transfer was slow, but eventually it got to professional sports. It made its way into the NFL and then Major League Baseball. It's been a cat-and-mouse game on testing ever since. Bottom line is, those drugs did work, they did advance performance, but it had horrible side effects."

Bush-Joseph cited the most extreme example of star NFL lineman Lyle Alzado of Broncos and Raiders fame, who died of heart disease linked to PED use. The jury is still out on the long-term effects of PED use in baseball. "The majority of athletes using PEDs used them because they were trying to recover quickly from injury, and it does help recovery," said Bush-Joseph, who also served eight years on MLB's medical advisory committee. "Then many realized if they take it, it doesn't help me with recovery, but it helps with gaining strength and body mass. It proved to be effective. There were estimates of 30 to 70 percent of players were doing something at some point."

PEDs skewed baseball's power numbers in a way never seen since Babe Ruth's emergence onto the scene as the game's greatest slugger in 1919-1920. The 50-homer barrier was breached just once—by the Reds' George Foster with 52—between 1965 and 1990. But in the middle of the steroid era, 60 bombs in a season was reached six times, three by the Cubs' Sammy Sosa in four seasons between 1998 and 2001. Sosa hit 50 in 2000. A science fiction–like 70—what sane baseball expert ever thought that level could be reached?—was achieved twice, by Mark McGwire in 1998 and by Barry Bonds for a record 73 in 2001.

Out-of-nowhere, one-season power explosions were recorded by players never projected to be prime sluggers.

Out-of-nowhere, one-season power explosions were recorded by players never projected to be prime sluggers. Orioles outfielder Brady Anderson slugged 50 homers in 1996. He had just two other seasons where he belted as many as 20. Diamondbacks outfielder Luis Gonzalez had been a basic 15-homer, sixth-place, supplemental left-handed hitter through most of the 1990s. He then jumped into the 20-homer range—okay, he was maturing as a hitter around 30—and then out of nowhere leaped to 57 homers (along with 142 RBIs) in 2001. Gonzalez then quieted back down into the 20s level with no hint of a repeat.

On Players Getting an Edge

SPITBALLING

"There's always going to be a continuous push-pull on players getting ahead of the game or getting ahead of testing techniques and enhancing their performance." —*Dr. Charles Bush-Joseph, associate director of the Rush Orthopedic Sports Medicine Fellowship*

Mandatory testing was delayed until after the 2002 Basic Agreement. Cynics will always accuse administrators of the game from Bud Selig down of turning a blind eye to the obvious use of PEDs as the game rode a revival thanks to the home-run derbies. But that's too simplistic of an analysis. A combination of inertia at the top and resistance to testing by a Players Association that had just endured baseball's worst-ever labor crisis caused the delay. Suspected users were repeatedly confronted without any true confessions.

On June 18, 2002, at Wrigley Field, Rangers manager Jerry Narron said Chicago fans on both sides of town were smart enough to know which of their star Cubs and White Sox were clean. A recording of Narron's comments was made and immediately rushed across the field to Sosa in the Cubs clubhouse. Sosa listened to the entire tape. "I'm not in the mood for that," he said. "I'm here to play baseball." Eventually, testing produced a minor dragnet of users. Earning the longest penalty in the majors was Alex Rodriguez, suspended for the entire 2014 season. But much seemed forgiven during Rodriguez's 2015 comeback.

That's the cycle of baseball. Forgiveness, then more of the age-old attempts to beat the system. As testing began in 2003, Sosa was nabbed by umpire Tim McClelland for using a corked bat in a game. A year later, a prominent Sosa teammate said as players stopped using PEDs, they resorted to corked bats. How did he know? "By the hollow sound they made" after they connected with pitches, came the reply. A decade after testing became imprinted in baseball, offense declined. A 50-homer producer will be a real standout. Teams are hoarding their young hitters, who are not being made available in trade-deadline deals.

One aspect never changes: the constant specter of failure and the temptations to get around its formidable barriers.

The Trade Deadline

Six More Weeks of the Flesh Market Boosts Interest in Baseball

NO. 33

Baseball innovator Branch Rickey (who signed Jackie Robinson and created the farm system) actually prompted baseball to take a big backward step in 1922.

Angered that the New York Yankees and Giants were able to load up with late-July trades bolstered by cash payments to weaker teams, then-Cardinals bossman Rickey rallied St. Louis civic organizations to protest the moves to Commissioner Kenesaw Mountain Landis. In response, Landis moved the mid-season trade deadline from August 1 back to June 15, forcing teams to the more complicated process of waivers—involving a system of team claims and pullbacks of players—to make deals after the earlier deadline.

Already in place were prohibitions against interleague deals during the season. Trades between the National League and American League were allowed only between November 21 and the end of the winter meetings until 1970, when the start of the flesh-market interleague period was moved up to five days after the end of the World Series. In 1977, a second offseason interleague period was established between February 15 and March 15, with the deadline extended to April 1 in 1981.

Many members of the baseball establishment did not like commerce between the leagues.

"Warren Giles, [1950s and 1960s] president of the National League, was a strong, strong proponent of not trading stars to the other league," said longtime baseball executive Roland

In 1998, Randy Johnson joined Lou Brock as a future
Hall of Famer dealt at the trade deadline.

Hemond, former GM of the White Sox and Orioles. "He was vehement that clubs would be cautious."

The restrictive interleague deadlines stimulated both action and fan interest in the winter meetings, such as Hemond's stunning acquisition of Dick Allen for the White Sox in exchange for Tommy John in 1971.

"I met [Dodgers GM] Al Campanis at the winter meetings," Hemond remembered. "He said, 'Roland, are you considering trading Tommy John?' We said, 'Yes, for the right deal.' Al mentioned Dick Allen. I said to [wife] Margo, 'Keep Al busy in the lobby so he doesn't go talk to anyone else.' I immediately went to find [White Sox manager] Chuck Tanner. He said, 'I love Dick Allen.' It was kind of spontaneous when it came about."

The winter meetings were chock full of such dazzling stories. But, overall, the restrictive deadlines hamstrung teams seeking to bolster their rosters when they established themselves as contenders in the second half of seasons. Fortunately, starting with the 1986 campaign, the trade deadline was moved back to July 31 with interleague trades permitted during the season. "It made a lot of sense," said Dallas Green, another prominent front-office veteran. "June was a pretty hectic month with the amateur draft. Having a [June 15] trade deadline was ridiculous in my opinion and I was glad to see it moved."

Deals that should have been completed were cut off at the pass with no way to keep talks going due to the artificially early deadlines, both during the season and at the winter meetings.

On Getting the Call That You've Been Traded

"I just thought it was my wife [who had called]. Then I was saddened when they told me it was [Cubs GM John] Holland. I thought I was either going to the minors or being traded. I gave Holland credit because he did it gently. He said he had made an 'arrangement.' He said he had 'transferred my contract.' . . . Finally, he said my contract had been transferred to the St. Louis Cardinals. I was consumed and overwhelmed with the reality I was still in the big leagues."
—*Hall of Famer Lou Brock, traded from the Cubs to the Cardinals on June 15, 1964*

SPITBALLING

"I was working for the Astros in 1978," recalled Gordon Lakey, now director of major-league scouting for the Phillies. "At the 1978 winter meetings in Orlando, the [interleague] trade deadline was at 9 a.m. We had a [prospective] deal to acquire Nolan Ryan from the Angels. At 9 a.m., there was no word from Buzzy [Bavasi, the Angels' GM] or anything. Buzzy was at the dog track at Daytona Beach with no intent to make the deal."

Now, with the restrictions and deadlines lifted, such deals could be consummated.

The new deadline has stimulated player movement and fan interest going into baseball's dog days while creating two tiers of teams—buyers and sellers. Teams give signals to their fans that they are going full-bore for the playoffs by acquiring big-name players by July 31. In contrast, their trading partners are waving the white flag, admitting they are out of the race and settling for young talent in return to re-boot.

The two biggest names to move on July 31 were Randy Johnson and Manny Ramirez. In 1998, the Mariners moved Johnson to the Astros, who provided quality compensation in Freddy Garcia, Carlos Guillen, and John Halama. The Big Unit struck out 116, allowing just 12 runs, in 84 innings for the 102-win Astros. But Houston did not reach the World Series even with their 6'10" southpaw. Exactly 10 years later, the Red Sox shed a clubhouse problem in Ramirez, who emerged as an energized centerpiece with the Dodgers. Ramirez batted .396 with 17 homers in the final two months, powering the Dodgers to their first postseason series victory in 20 years. However, LA also fell short of the World Series.

Some trading seasons are busier than others. In 2000, 2001, and 2006, teams made 42 trades each between June 1 and July 31. When Johnson moved to Houston, he was among 40 deals during that time period. Major League Baseball also has improved the marketing of the trade deadline. In the 1990s, the deadline was midnight July 31, causing some deals to miss newspaper deadlines and the earlier editions of ESPN's *SportsCenter*. More recently, the deadline has been moved up to mid-afternoon, better to make a big production out of the flesh market for both ESPN and the game's own MLB Network.

Some trading seasons are busier than others. In 2000, 2001, and 2006, teams made 42 trades each between June 1 and July 31.

Some believe August 15 would be a more realistic deadline. A few even suggest August 31, now the deadline for acquiring players on waivers to be eligible for postseason play, would be warranted. The second wild card was instituted on Commissioner Bud Selig's watch. But successor Rob Manfred verbalized the need to support player movement via a later deadline necessitated by an increased potential playoff field of teams.

Frank Robinson

Integrating Baseball's Managerial Ranks

When Frank Robinson made out his Cleveland Indians lineup on April 8, 1975, he became the majors' first black manager. But while the intense Robinson had broken the game's managerial color line, it would not soon result in a whole series of skippers of color.

He's a trailblazer nonetheless, and as baseball is a slow-to-change world, only a select few of its game changers worked rapidly. Like Larry Doby serving as the first African-American player on both the Indians in 1948 and the Detroit Tigers in 1959, Robinson ended up as the first black manager for the San Francisco Giants and Baltimore Orioles. Felipe Alou managed the Montreal Expos in the 1990s, so Robinson was not the first manager of color in that franchise's history when he was hired in 2002 and shepherded the franchise through its relocation to Washington, DC, as the Nationals. Eventually and thankfully, the very concept of a black or Latin manager did not merit special notice as baseball finally came around.

The countdown to the first black manager, though, had dragged out so long that when Robinson finally was named Indians manager immediately after the 1974 season, the hype over his debut had the entire offseason to percolate. A mob of 56,715 and a national media throng turned out at Municipal Stadium on Opening Day against the Yankees.

Still active as a player, Robinson slotted himself second in the batting order as DH between Oscar Gamble and George Hendrick. Never known as a "flair" guy in his hard-nosed

NO. 34

Frank Robinson (right) near the peak of his career
as a Cincinnati Red with popular Cubs coach
Verlon "Rube" Walker at Wrigley Field

career, Robinson injected all the glory you could imagine with a homer in his first at-bat off Yankees right-hander Doc Medich. He'd go on to belt the final 12 of his 586 career homers as player-manager over 85 games in the 1975 and 1976 seasons.

Several prominent African Americans who followed Robinson's path from player to coach and/or manager have since confessed that the pioneer seemed an unlikely managerial color-line breaker. Willie Mays, Ernie Banks, and Maury Wills were considered more plausible candidates.

"Back in the day, when Robinson played, he was a kind of different personality than most. Very intense," said ex–first baseman Cecil Cooper, who became the Houston Astros' first black manager from 2007 to 2009. Due to his "demeanor" and "fiery spirit," Robinson also was not foremost in the mind of 1970s outfielder Gene Clines, who went on to coach with the Cubs, Astros, Mariners, Brewers, and Giants.

Instead, said Clines, "The person who came into my mind right away because of his character and demeanor was Vada Pinson. Vada was a very laid back–type guy. Another guy who was a leader by example. I thought he had the right temperament to handle that job. The personality difference between him [Robinson] was like night and day."

Some believed the fiery Jackie Robinson would be a second-time trailblazer as a manager, but they were far too optimistic on the timetable. An October 27, 1951, *Collier's* magazine, projecting ahead to a fictionalized world of 1960, referred to "Brooklyn Dodgers manager Jackie Robinson." The publication was not only way off on Robinson, but also the concept of a Brooklyn without the Dodgers.

The majors did not have a black coach until the Cubs' Buck O'Neil in 1962. But in the madcap "College of Coaches" system of the day, O'Neil was not allowed to assume the rotating

On Breaking a New Racial Barrier

"I am extremely proud and pleased. But I will be more pleased the day I can look over at the third base line and see a black man as manager." –*Jackie Robinson, at his final public appearance, Game 2 of the 1972 World Series*

SPITBALLING

"head coach" position. Nor was he allowed to coach third base, a prohibition that affected the first generation of black coaches like the Dodgers' Jim Gilliam, the Yankees' Elston Howard, and the Expos' Larry Doby. Gilliam had a five-year head start on Tommy Lasorda on the Dodgers' coaching lines, but Lasorda ended up at third and the successor to 22-year manager Walter Alston late in 1976. Belying their Robinson legacy, after the long tenures of white managers Alston and Lasorda, the Dodgers hired seven more without employing a person of color.

Yogi Berra would have had a field day with the déjà vu concept of Bill Veeck and Doby. Just as Veeck anointed Doby the second African-American player in the majors in 1947, he hired him as the second black manager to replace Bob Lemon with the White Sox 74 games into the 1978 season. Doby only lasted the balance of the season and did not manage again.

Some believed the fiery Jackie Robinson would be a second-time trailblazer as a manager, but they were far too optimistic on the timetable.

Cito Gaston racked up the next big managerial achievement as the first African American to win a World Series via back-to-back achievements with the Toronto Blue Jays in 1992-93. But on the flip side, managers of color had to endure the usual sorrows in the ultimate game of failure. The baseball gods don't discriminate in capricious and unfair outcomes.

In his third managing job with Baltimore, Frank Robinson—replacing the fired Cal Ripken Sr.—had to endure the final 15 games of an astounding season-opening 21-game losing streak in 1988. Dusty Baker was one game away from a series win two years in a row—the World Series with the Giants with a 3–2 lead in 2002 and the National League Championship Series with the Cubs with a 3–1 lead in 2003—and came up empty. The Giants coughed up a 5–0 seventh-inning lead in Game 6, while the "Bartman Game" with a 3–0 lead and five outs to go in Game 6 with the Cubs is now baseball legend. Meanwhile, Felipe Alou skippered the 74-40 Montreal Expos in 1994 when the strike wiped out the remainder of the season. Following in Alou's stead, Latin managers have had mixed success. The fact English was not their first language did not stop general managers' hiring plans once the barriers were broken. In fact, in Ozzie Guillen's case, his mouth, via English or Spanish, got the Venezuelan native into trouble starting the year after he ranked as the first Latin manager to win a World Series with the White Sox in 2005. Guillen was mandated sensitivity training by commissioner Bud Selig for a gay slur directed against a sports columnist. He virtually talked his way out of the Chicago job by 2011, migrated to the Marlins, and then angered the masses with seemingly favorable comments about Fidel Castro. Cashiered after just one season in Miami, Guillen has not managed ever since.

Indeed, managers—of any race or ethnicity—are hired to be fired.

Hank Aaron
From Underexposed Star to National Hero Standing beside the Babe

Henry Aaron achieved national-hero status and the love of an entire country that still radiates more than four decades after he broke Babe Ruth's all-time home-run mark, arguably all sports' most prestigious record.

Aaron's record-busting homer into the Fulton County Stadium left field bullpen, caught by reliever Tom House, on April 8, 1974, is one of the most replayed moments in sports history. And leave it to baseball poet laureate Vin Scully to ad-lib the feat's true impact on Los Angeles's KABC-Radio after letting the crowd roar for more than 90 seconds following the homer:

NO. **35**

> *"What a marvelous moment for baseball . . . What a marvelous moment for Atlanta and the state of Georgia . . . What a marvelous moment for the country . . . A black man is getting a standing ovation in the Deep South for breaking a record of an all-time baseball idol. And it is a great moment for all of us . . . and particularly for Henry Aaron. . . . And for the first time in a long time, that poker face in Aaron shows the tremendous strain and relief of what it must have been like to live with for the past several months."*

The story was rooted in Aaron's journey as one of baseball's top players through two small markets—Milwaukee and Atlanta—starting in 1954 and then his "discovery" by the casual fan and non-baseball rooter as he lined up Ruth in his sights starting in 1970. All-time greatness came through a multi-year quest in which Aaron triumphed over racism, displaying the ultimate grace under fire.

Reggie Jackson and Hank Aaron (right) at the dedication ceremony for the Hank Aaron Boyhood Home Museum at the Hank Aaron Stadium, Mobile, Alabama

Over his career, Aaron was as good a player as Willie Mays. But the "Say-Hey Kid" had the advantage of playing in media-capital New York with the Giants, having the voluble manager Leo Durocher as his publicity man, and making perhaps the greatest catch in World Series history on the Indians' Vic Wertz in 1954. Meanwhile, Aaron debuted in folksy small-market Milwaukee in 1954, the same year as Mays's breakthrough season. His accomplishments should have made Aaron a national sensation. He won the NL batting title with .328 at age 22 in 1956. His walk-off homer against the Cardinals' Billy Muffett in the 11th inning clinched the NL pennant for the Braves on September 23, 1957, topping off his Most Valuable Player campaign in which he paced the league with 44 homers and 132 RBIs to go along with a .322 mark. Aaron led the NL in homers and RBIs four times each.

While the shift to Atlanta in 1966 did not dramatically raise the modest Aaron's profile, it positioned him better for the assault on the all-time record. Fulton County Stadium's friendly fences along with hot, humid weather and foothill-level altitude (around 1,000 feet above sea level) made for better home-run conditions. Aaron transformed himself into a pull hitter, stepping up the power pace in late career. He amassed a career high of 47 homers in 1971. That season included his 600th homer. Projections began to center on Aaron as the man who could pass Ruth. Aaron became encased in the fishbowl for good in 1973. All eyes were trained on his every move as the countdown to Ruth's 715 began in earnest. Every ballpark stop on each road trip became a media sensation with Aaron trying to accommodate all comers. Fans accorded him standing ovations and mobbed him everywhere.

Interestingly, Fulton County Stadium was the only venue not caught up in the hoopla. The '73 Braves drew just 800,000. Cut to behind the scenes: The haters who made Robinson's break-in season in 1947 a challenge for even the most thick-skinned man had not disappeared 26 years later. Aaron was deluged with hate mail with the most vile racist epithets and constant death threats. "You know he still has all that mail," 1970s Braves announcer Milo Hamilton said in an interview before he passed away in September 2015. Aaron directed secretary Carla Koplin to save the hate letters law enforcement authorities did not need for investigations.

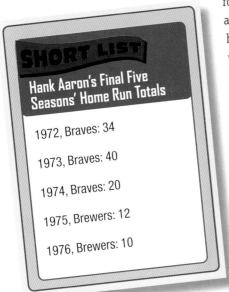

SHORT LIST

Hank Aaron's Final Five Seasons' Home Run Totals

1972, Braves: 34

1973, Braves: 40

1974, Braves: 20

1975, Brewers: 12

1976, Brewers: 10

During his pursuit of Ruth, Aaron had real reason to fear for his safety and his family's. Atlanta police detective Calvin Wardlaw was assigned to shadow Aaron's home as his bodyguard. The FBI watched over his family members, taking seriously a kidnapping threat against daughter Gaile Aaron at Fisk University. G-men disguised as campus workers were deployed all over campus. In his 1991 autobiography *I Had A Hammer* with Lonnie Wheeler, Aaron described fighting off despair with the nasty letters. "As the hate mail piled up," he wrote, "I became more and more intent on breaking the record and shoving it in the ugly faces of those bigots. I'm sure it made me a better hitter."

But publicity over the hateful messages turned the tide toward the positive, and the letter writers became overwhelmingly supportive. Koplin received 3,000 letters a day. The US Postal Service gave Aaron a plaque for receiving the most letters—930,000—of any non-politician in the country in 1973. Dinah Shore was runner-up with 60,000. The majority of the United States hopped on Aaron's journey and counted down.

The US Postal Service gave Aaron a plaque for receiving the most letters—930,000—of any non-politician in the country in 1973.

"Never did it come out to the point where you felt like he was a bitter man," said Reds announcer Marty Brennaman, whose first big-league game in the booth was at Riverfront Stadium on Opening Day, April 4, 1974. Aaron wasted no time tying Ruth with a three-run homer in the first off Jack Billingham. In the crowd was Vice President Gerald R. Ford, just four months away from assuming the presidency upon the resignation of Richard M. Nixon.

Commissioner Bowie Kuhn mandated Aaron play two of the three games in the opening series in Cincinnati. So, almost on cue, Aaron got No. 715 three nights later in Atlanta before a massive national TV audience.

His journey was complete, in more ways than one. Aaron was part of the generation of African-American players who followed Jackie Robinson while he still played, and to whom Robinson was able to impart the wisdom of his own trials by fire. Now that generation became the stewards of the game, possessor of many of the records and its most cherished symbols.

Aaron is baseball's elder statesman. He is still mobbed wherever he goes, is given standing ovations. People still hang on his words. With 755 homers, seven short of Barry Bonds's official record, he is still considered the greatest sultan of swat.

"With all due respect to others involved, I'll go to the grave feeling like Henry Aaron is the all-time home-run king," said Brennaman. "Despite the fact the numbers would indicate Barry Bonds, Aaron did it clean and Bonds didn't.

"I'm not so sure Henry Aaron isn't the greatest living baseball player of all of them."

Michael Jordan

"Be Like Mike" Lures Kids Away from Baseball

Baseball entered the 1980s with its traditional appeal to kids relatively intact.

To be sure, the NFL had made huge inroads on the national pastime. Sunday football TV viewing had become habit with the lifting of the old home blackout rule in 1973 dramatically increasing the number of games on the tube. Baseball began yielding both weekend afternoons to football by scheduling postseason games around pro and college gridiron telecasts.

But baseball remained relatively strong at the grassroots. Little League participation was still growing. Minority participation at the youth level, bubbling up to big-league destinations, was relatively healthy. In the mid-1970s, 27 percent of big leaguers were African-American. Baseball was still perceived as a destination sport.

Then came the No. 3 pick in the 1984 NBA draft. Passing up taking Sam Bowie, who would have filled a more crying need at center, the woebegone Chicago Bulls nabbed high-flying, NCAA championship–experienced Michael Jordan out of North Carolina. He had an explosive game played above the court—up to and above rim level—and an unparalleled will to win. The dead-eye, late-game mid-range jump shot and defensive shutdown prowess would be added later.

Jordan had magnetism from the get-go. He became a pied piper. What was a trickle of an attraction when Magic Johnson's all-around game powered the Lakers to an NBA title in 1980 became a torrent as Jordan became sports' most transcendent star by his third season

Michael Jordan lured countless young athletes to basketball from their traditional baseball moorings.

in 1986-87, ranking fifth all time in points per game at 37.1. Then he followed up with a ninth-ranked 35 per game and won the 1988 All-Star Game Slam Dunk competition. The minority-community's youthful allegiance to baseball began to decline in earnest.

Other factors contributed. The high cost of traveling teams, the increase in playing-field dimensions that discourage less-talented players after Little League, and the lack of full-ride college baseball scholarships presented successive choke points to minority participation and advancement in the game. But Jordan was so appealing as an emergent star that an overheated man once walked away from a Chicago Stadium game late on a 1989 night yelling "Black Jesus! Black Jesus!" after witnessing another Jordan virtuoso performance on and above the court.

Baseball had no comparable appealing all-timer to counter Jordan's lure. Barry Bonds, exquisitely talented, petulantly refused to serve as the game's role model. Jordan complemented an all-around game that nudged the Bulls to six NBA titles starting in 1991 with a commercial persona unmatched in late 20th century America. The "be like Mike" campaigns, led by Nike and his Air Jordans shoes, won the loyalty of millions of kids. Jordan seemed natural, and his posse was savvy. Endorsement impresario David Falk and Jordan's family positioned him as an all-American type who did not endorse Japanese companies, which at the time encroached on and then supplanted many domestic products as best-sellers.

"I may be fortunate to be respected, to show positive role-model traits," Jordan told *Sport* magazine during the 1989-90 season. "Everybody's benefitting from this, even though I didn't ask to be put in this position. It's something I've accepted."

Eventually, Jordan would be shown to have feet of clay like any other big-name athlete. But he deposited enough in the bank of public goodwill to become the most popular athlete of his time and convert countless kids to would-be Jordans. In the first half of his career, he was amazingly accessible for sports' biggest name, addressing reporters by first names, looking at them squarely in the eye and composing complete thoughts. "I get tired of [media] every now and then, but I know how to get rid of my frustrations without doing it against other people," Jordan said. "Either I do it playing basketball or I take it home."

By 2006, the number of African-American big-league players had dropped to 8.6 percent.

The long-term effects of the allure of Jordan and the NBA could be shown at both the top and entry-level parts of baseball. By 2006, the number of African-American big-league players had dropped to 8.6 percent. In 2014, the famed Jackie Robinson West Little League program on Chicago's South Side had 300 kids enrolled—half the 1990 number.

Amazingly, Jordan was a forerunner of baseball's exodus. He was a star North Carolina

On Jordan's Baseball Career

"Baseball's a skills sport. You don't have to be a great athlete. But you do have to have specific skills. Ninety-nine-point-nine percent of players in the NBA could not play baseball at the A level. Michael Jordan impressed me so much to be out of baseball as long as he was and come back to play baseball at the Double-A level, and hit .202. Which is considered [by regular standards] a total failure, but I think that was unbelievably impressive."
—*Cincinnati Reds bench coach Jim Riggleman*

SPITBALLING

Little Leaguer who initially was cut from his high school basketball team. Even after mastering basketball like nobody else, he never forgot his roots in the game. In the spring of 1993, Falk said Jordan's long-term goal was to play pro baseball when he retired. The timetable rapidly advanced after Jordan's father, James Jordan, was murdered in the summer of '93, and Jordan announced what turned out to be a one-and-a-half-season retirement from the Bulls.

Three years earlier, Jordan's supreme athletic confidence was verbalized: "Yeah, if I put my mind to it, I could play any sport that I chose." He seemed to refer to advancing to the pro level of golf, then his spare-time passion. But in the winter of 1993-94, he applied that philosophy to playing minor-league baseball in the White Sox farm system.

Jordan shifted attention to the Double-A Southern League in a manner no one else could fashion. His 1994 season for the Birmingham Barons became the feel-good story of a year marred by baseball's worst-ever strike. He possessed sufficient residual baseball skills to be able to get a hit one of every five times at-bat in '94 when Jordan scratched his baseball itch. He avoided being caught up in the replacement-player issue in spring training 1995 by announcing his return to the Bulls with a succinct message: "I'm back." The brief bump baseball might have enjoyed was dissipated by the strike and three more Jordan-led Bulls championships between 1996 and 1998.

In essence, Jordan was the Babe Ruth of his generation. The difference was that he played basketball, not baseball. The grand ol' game—if it can ever accomplish the feat—will require decades to reverse the talent outflow thanks to Jordan's once-in-a-lifetime career.

Barry Bonds
Declining the Role Model Job

The job of baseball role model for minority youths, if not the entire baseball-playing population, was wide open as the 1980s matured.

The great Hall of Fame–bound African-American players such as Hank Aaron, Willie Mays, Frank Robinson, and Bob Gibson had long retired. Someone with consummate skills combined with appealing personality was needed to take the stage. Although youth participation in the African-American community was still strong as the 80s commenced, competition for their loyalties and choice of sports began encroaching through an all-powerful NFL and the superstardom of first Magic Johnson, then Michael Jordan.

NO. 37

The perfect man for the job seemed to be Barry Lamar Bonds, initially a lithe, five-tool outfielder with the Pittsburgh Pirates. He came from royal baseball bloodlines, with dad Bobby Bonds a 30-30 star who broke into the Giants' outfield in 1968 next to Mays. The younger Bonds was even a distant cousin of Reggie Jackson. He was naturally articulate and knew his way around the majors, having grown up around clubhouses.

But as Bonds established himself as a superstar, then mined free-agent gold with the Giants—his family's ancestral team—he declined to take on the leadership mantle. Instead, Bonds developed an often-petulant image, keeping the media, and in translation the fans, at bay. By mid-summer of 1996, he was baseball's greatest all-around player, with numbers projecting to all-time great status and sure Hall of Fame induction. He could easily be compared to Ted Williams in his mastery as a left-handed hitter. Yet few felt a warmth and natural pull toward Bonds due to his off-putting attitude that exceeded Williams's famed antipathy toward sportswriters. Interestingly, Bonds explained why he developed his

By 2000, Barry Bonds, the former five-tool player looked a lot different than his slim, trim photo from his Pittsburgh Pirates days at the cusp of the 1990s.

persona in a candid, but ultimately bizarre stream of consciousness one day in the visitors' dugout at Wrigley Field. Here is the transcription of Bonds on Bonds, recorded July 30, 1996, two years before he perked up due to the Sosa-McGwire home-run derby:

The younger Bonds was even a distant cousin of Reggie Jackson. He was naturally articulate and knew his way around the majors, having grown up around clubhouses.

"I wasn't the golden child, so I wasn't picked to be one. Not too many famous children of famous people are. Always the marketable person, the ones who are loved in society, are the unknown names. They're the ones that shocked people by surprise.

"How many fathers' children have become the marketable stars, the public figures in society? None. You can't think of any except [Ken] Griffey, Jr. And his father wasn't the main guy on the [Big] Red Machine. He was a great baseball player, he was part of the [Big] Red Machine. But Johnny Bench, Pete Rose and all them overshadowed him publicly with all the media.

"We of famous parents aren't the golden child. The Michael Jordans, The Magic Johnsons, the Shaquille O'Neals are the name people. The Joe Montanas, Muhammad Alis, they're the unknown, they take the world by surprise."

The question was put to Bonds point-blank: Do you want to be the role model for baseball?

"I feel I can," he said. "I don't see why I couldn't. What happened to me is the fact I rebelled against the media. I got a cousin named Reggie Smith, I got a cousin named Reggie Jackson. I got a godfather named Willie Mays. I have a father named Bobby Bonds. When you're a young kid trying to make it and you're going through situations like: can you be Mr. October like your cousin, will you ever be as great as your godfather, will you ever do 30-30 like your father? And the media comes up to you and says, 'Oops, Bobby, oops, Barry, I mean, oh I relate to your father.'

"The media never grasps Barry Bonds. That's where our misunderstanding came in. That's where the tangles came in. That's when the battle came in. As much as I wanted to mingle when I first started in my career in the minor leagues when I was so accessible, I came to them with open arms. They never embraced Barry, they always embraced the son of great family. I rebelled against them. That was my own mistake. You can't tell a young child you're making a mistake at the time. You're not mature enough to understand and see it. The only thing you want is to embrace you as a person, as a human being. I was never embraced by the media for what I was doing."

As a hint of things to come, Bonds kept comparing himself to sports' greatest of the day. He came off bearing an apparent inferiority complex.

"When Michael Jordan makes a great move, it's like, 'Oh, Michael!' When Dennis Rodman makes a great rebound, 'Oh, Dennis Rodman.' When Ken Griffey Jr. hits a home run, it's 'Ken Griffey Jr.' When Barry Bonds does something, it's, 'Bobby, oops, I mean Barry, but I relate to his father or godfather, or he does things just like his godfather . . . but he hasn't been able to come through in the playoffs like his cousin Reggie.' No one has been able to embrace me. I never really gave them the time back. I tried to at the beginning. But I refuse to because I think it's their turn."

Once the tape recorder was turned off, Bonds's interviewer had a thought, posed directly to the superstar. He recalled the pleasant, choreographed Jordan personality that sold millions of Nikes and other products."Barry, why can't you be like Mike? There's millions of dollars to be made?" asked the interviewer. Bonds had no reaction.

The interview, stunning even when reviewed two decades later, helps explain what happened starting three years later. Dripping with envy in his candor that afternoon, Bonds hardly changed his tune when Mark McGwire and Sammy Sosa staged their artificially boosted home-run chase in 1998. Bonds was not going to be left out of the glory-seeking no matter what it took.

Every bit of evidence going forward showed Bonds was linked to performance-enhancing drugs. The recriminations quickly followed Bonds's 73-homer outburst in 2001 that obliterated McGwire's three-year-old mark of 70. And a collective baseball nation held its nose in 2007 when Bonds broke Henry Aaron's lifetime 755-homer mark to finish seven ahead of Hammerin' Hank. The wayward role model only thought as far ahead as 500 homers in 1996. Given his career production pace at the time, he might have reached the 700-ballpark on his natural talents without any chemical pumping-up. He would have been a perfect role model to corral minority youths to baseball. Yet as his own narrative proves, Barry Bonds never felt the world gave him the credit due when it could have or should have been the other way around—Bonds reaching out to keep the masses in baseball's fold.

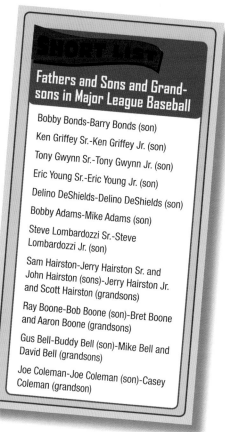

SHORTLIST

Fathers and Sons and Grandsons in Major League Baseball

Bobby Bonds-Barry Bonds (son)

Ken Griffey Sr.-Ken Griffey Jr. (son)

Tony Gwynn Sr.-Tony Gwynn Jr. (son)

Eric Young Sr.-Eric Young Jr. (son)

Delino DeShields-Delino DeShields (son)

Bobby Adams-Mike Adams (son)

Steve Lombardozzi Sr.-Steve Lombardozzi Jr. (son)

Sam Hairston-Jerry Hairston Sr. and John Hairston (sons)-Jerry Hairston Jr. and Scott Hairston (grandsons)

Ray Boone-Bob Boone (son)-Bret Boone and Aaron Boone (grandsons)

Gus Bell-Buddy Bell (son)-Mike Bell and David Bell (grandsons)

Joe Coleman-Joe Coleman (son)-Casey Coleman (grandson)

Sabermetrics

New Stats and Old-Fashioned Scouting Try to Coexist

Who was a better player based on RBIs, or ERAs, or any old-school statistical measurement? Ted Williams's decision to play the second game of a doubleheader on the final day of the 1941 season rather than sit on a batting average that would be rounded to .400 was a leader in umpteen baseball stories based on the crunching of numbers.

NO.  38

But a new generation of statistics has jumped front and center in the game—sabermetrics. Understanding the dizzying sets of figures seems to require high SAT scores in math, but they now battle for the hearts and minds of the lords of the realm with traditional eyeball analysis of players and knowledge of their personalities. Baseball the numbers game was also a people sport, and the two factors were always interrelated.

The traditional scoreboard listings of box scores and league leaders is now supplemented with tables of catchy acronyms. WAR (Wins Over Replacement) rankings for hitters and pitchers and WHIP (Walks and Hits to Innings Pitched) stats are easily available. Sabermetrics analysts have maximum prestige in the game, with the best-selling book and Hollywood glamorization of Athletics numbers trailblazer Billy Beane leading the way via *Moneyball*. And in the battle of well-guarded computer analysis of this brave new world, baseball experienced its first hacking scandal involving the Cardinals and Astros.

"Those who attack sabermetrics, claiming those who use advanced metrics are simply holed up in basements not enjoying the game, are simply wrong," said Al Yellon, managing editor of the popular *BleedCubbieBlue.com* website. A baseball fan since 1963, Yellon was raised on traditional numbers, yet has totally embraced sabermetrics as a tool on the job.

Oakland Athletics general manager Billy Beane was
an avid reader of sabermetrics pioneer Bill James.

"Bill James began the sabermetric revolution in the early 1980s, and he did so by asking questions about the game, wanting to understand it better," Yellon added. "That led to the invention of new ways of analyzing baseball, helped by the fact that most of us now have in our pockets devices with more computing power than computers in huge rooms had 40 years ago."

Front offices were being increasingly stocked by twentysomething and thirtysomething executives from business, not baseball backgrounds.

James is the godfather of sabermetrics, also derived from an acronym—SABR (Society for American Baseball Research). A 1970s boiler-room attendant at the Stokely Van Kamp pork and beans plant in Lawrence in his native Kansas, James's quizzical mind on and off the job questioned conventional baseball statistics as not telling the entire story, or the wrong story. In the process of authoring his annual *Baseball Abstract*, he became the first in a series of new-age baseball analysts who hailed from nontraditional backgrounds.

When James was finally brought into the front office as senior baseball operations advisor to the Red Sox in 2002, he was already behind the curve. Front offices were being increasingly stocked by twentysomething and thirtysomething executives from business, not baseball backgrounds.

One of the young turks, Theo Epstein, had been consuming James's output for nearly two decades when he advanced to the Red Sox GM job at 28. He became a James fan in fourth grade in Brookline, Massachusetts.

Given control of a team, Epstein mandated state-of-the-art numbers crunching. His computer system at Fenway Park was nicknamed "Carmine." When he moved on to the Cubs, his baseball operations redoubt was considered a maximum-security operation.

On Sabermetrics versus Scouting

"I talked [in 2014] to a GM for a ballclub in the NL East I have great respect for, and I asked him on a scale from 1 to 100 percent, how much do you devote to sabermetrics? He said, 'I'm an old-school guy, 75 percent I devote to accepting the word of people who have devoted their lives to scouting talent and 25 percent to sabermetrics.'" —*Marty Brennaman, Cincinnati Reds radio broadcaster*

SPITBALLING

James's works had first made inroads into organized baseball by the 1990s, and he quietly worked as a consultant to three big-league teams. Oakland Athletics GM Sandy Alderson was an early devotee. Young Alderson deputy and successor Billy Beane, a voracious *Abstract* reader, expanded the consciousness of his front office by the turn of the millennium as the basis for *Moneyball*, the book by Michael Lewis. On-base percentage, formerly a secondary analytical tool to batting average, now became a prime measuring stick of a hitter's true effectiveness. Sabermetrics steadily expanded from that well-publicized base.

"This sort of statistical analysis has helped people understand baseball better and why 'traditional' statistics, while useful, don't tell the whole story," Yellon said. "RBIs, for example, are useful—but also team-dependent, because you don't know how well a so-called 'RBI man' is doing unless you know how many men are getting on base ahead of him, how many opportunities he has, how well he does in specific situations, etc. ERA is useful, but FIP [Fielding-Independent Pitching] has been created to tell the story of a pitcher's performance that's due to his pitching, not how well his fielders do behind him. UZR [Ultimate Zone Rating] tells us far more about fielders than errors can, though it likely needs more tweaking. All of these things can now be known where they weren't before, and they're not used just to crunch numbers, they're used by front offices to help them put together better teams."

The number that seems to have become first among equals in sabermetrics is WAR. "Perhaps the best, although also the most controversial, of the new metrics is WAR," said Yellon. "It's designed to set a baseline for what a 'replacement player'—in other words, someone who would be called up from the minor leagues or be acquired off the waiver wire— would do 'replacing' a regular—[what he] would contribute to a team, and state by various calculations how many wins a player would add to a team's total."

Moneyball's nararative suggested a conflict between the statistical revolution and traditional methods of scouting. The scouts gauge makeup and character, getting to know the environment in which their players operate, wrangling invitations into their homes to measure the kind of upbringing they experienced.

"I use some of these new [metrics], but overall I try to scout for character," said Bill Bryk, a scout since 1979 and special assistant to the Arizona Diamondbacks general manager.

The Atlanta Braves have been using character as a prime measuring stick in forging consistent contenders as far back as the early 1990s, in spite of drafting behind most other teams due to its top-shelf records.

Sabermetrics changed the game, to be sure. But it can never change the need for personal baseball personnel interaction.

George Steinbrenner

"The Boss" Creates Two Tiers of Baseball Teams

NO. 39

Rich and semi-poor teams have always existed in baseball, but the divide was never so great as when bombastic Yankees owner George Steinbrenner used the motherlode of revenue available in the nation's largest market to fuel his desire to win.

All the while Steinbrenner hired free agents and fired managers, namely Billy Martin, in a constantly revolving door, the gap between haves and have-nots grew to the point where commissioner Bud Selig proposed cutting the Minnesota Twins and Montreal Expos. Thankfully, the franchise-chopping never did take place, and both the Twins and Expos (as the reborn Washington Nationals) developed into contenders. The Kansas City Royals, another small-market laggard, suddenly revived in 2014 with entertaining homegrown players and a healthy dash of speed and defense. Mandated revenue sharing to benefit the smaller-market teams was instituted in 2002.

Although the lower-revenue teams proved they could build winners, Steinbrenner still possessed a huge advantage, one shared by his John Henry–led arch-rivals in Boston and the new mega-rich Guggenheim Partners, Los Angeles Dodgers owners.

Steinbrenner revived the formerly dynastic franchise after a decade-long slumber with his 1973 purchase from CBS. Son of a Cleveland shipbuilder and a former college football assistant coach, he had dabbled in basketball-team ownership and missed out on landing an NBA franchise for his hometown. Later he'd be a minority owner of the Chicago Bulls in the pre–Michael Jordan days. Steinbrenner displayed the impetus for outspending all rivals

George Steinbrenner helped widen the financial gap between big- and small-market teams with his regional TV deals in New York.

for big-name players when Catfish Hunter was declared a free agent after the 1974 season due to Oakland owner Charlie Finley's contractual bumbling. Steinbrenner tendered Hunter a five-year, $3.35 million contract, richest in baseball history to that date. That only gave fodder to traditionalists demanding the preservation of the reserve clause, then under assault. "Most of his rival owners shrieked in terror when Marvin [Miller] freed the players in the Seitz decision," said former longtime *New York Daily News* baseball writer Bill Madden, who covered Steinbrenner up-close-and-personal much of his ownership tenure. "George was a visionary as far as I was concerned in free agency. He saw how quickly he could build a winning team out of free agency."

As soon as free-agent pioneer Andy Messersmith was cleared to offer his services to the highest bidder during the spring of 1976, Steinbrenner was first in line. Messersmith agreed to a four-year, $1 million deal, but a dispute over deferred money caused the deal to be voided by commissioner Bowie Kuhn. Messersmith instead signed with Braves owner Ted Turner, another baseball neophyte who jumped all over free agency.

Soon Steinbrenner went after even bigger fish. "The way I see it, we need a cleanup hitter and we also need a star," he told Billy Martin and GM Gabe Paul after the 1976 season. The statement, as telling as any about Steinbrenner, was recalled in Madden's seminal 2010 biography, *Steinbrenner*. Jackson was the straw that stirred the drink for the 1976 inaugural free-agent class. Steinbrenner quenched his thirst to the tune of $2.96 million for five years. "He absolutely used free agency," said Hall of Famer Goose Gossage, Steinbrenner's closer of the era. "Not only did [the players] use it for gaining more money, but George took advantage of free agency to build a ballclub and put all the money back in to the team. George knew what the Yankees stood for. He had more influence on the way the game is than any single man but Marvin Miller. Both of them belong in the Hall of Fame."

Intent on replacing Jackson in the early 1980s, he signed Dave Winfield for a 10-year, $15 million payout. Steinbrenner also landed a post-surgical Tommy John, a great deal when he won 43 games his first two Yankees seasons. He also obtained "Man of Steal" Rickey Henderson via a seven-player trade with Oakland.

Steinbrenner kept raising the salary bar, forcing

Top Five Team Payrolls in 2010, the Year George Steinbrenner Died

Yankees $206,333,389

Red Sox $162,747,333

Cubs $146,859,000

Phillies $141,927,381

Mets $132,701,445

big- and middle-market teams to try to follow suit. Small-market Kansas City and Minnesota won World Series in 1985, 1987, and 1991, but the gap in the ability to spend was getting wider. The Royals and Twins, among others, soon dropped into long periods of also-ran status, unable to compete for top free-agents while being forced to let many of their own homegrown stars walk when their big paydays were due.

Top market cable-TV revenues helped bankroll Steinbrenner's splurges. He got $6.7 million a year on SportsChannel starting in 1983. Five years later, the Yankees triggered a clause to buy out their SportsChannel deal and landed the gold for nearly $500 million over 12 years from Madison Square Garden (MSG) Network. Eventually, the Yankees created their own cable carrier—YES (Yankees Entertainment and Sports Network). Steinbrenner's coffers were bulging like those of no other team.

Steinbrenner kept raising the salary bar, forcing big- and middle-market teams to try to follow suit.

"Where George was really a game changer was in television," said Madden. "Nobody thought anybody would get that kind of money. MSG was willing to get George whatever he wanted to get the Yankees. He parlayed that deal into forming his own network. That to me was where George was a revolutionary in baseball and probably deserves to be in the Hall of Fame on that alone. . . . That to me was as big a game changer as any owner in baseball."

Having moved past two suspensions from ownership, Steinbrenner finally listened to his baseball people and allowed his farm products to become mainstay Yankees rather than trade bait. The core of Derek Jeter, Bernie Williams, Mariano Rivera, Andy Pettitte, and Jorge Posada comprised the latest dynasty with four World Series titles in five years between 1996 and 2000. All but Williams were still around, and productive, for another championship in 2009. The homegrown centerpieces were actually a design for Yankees rivals to even the score. In an era of skyrocketing payrolls, retaining the majority of one's best prospects—especially hitters in a more pitching-dominated, post-PEDs landscape—became a more common strategy.

In 2001, the Red Sox and Dodgers joined the Yankees as the first three teams sporting $100 million payrolls. The Yankees passed the $200 million mark in 2008. Amazingly, the team fell to second in 2014, $32 million behind the Dodgers' $235 million, as a result of the Guggenheim group's mass transfusion of cash into Chavez Ravine. Steinbrenner's family, running the team since The Boss's 2010 death, now has a gilded competitor in Tinseltown.

Could another true game changer be at hand? If it is, then it has to go a long way to unwind the grab for gold that George Steinbrenner unleashed and paced most of the way until his death in 2010.

Steel and Concrete Ballparks

The Old That Would Become New Again

Baseball thrived during the construction boom before and after World War I, as steel and concrete ballparks dramatically increased their rickety predecessors' seating capacities and became their team's lasting identifications.

Several of these ballparks actually were built to last. With a lot of ongoing TLC and major renovations, Fenway Park and Wrigley Field survived to celebrate their centennials in the past decade and stand as the most beloved symbols of quaintness and traditionalism.

Most of the vintage ballparks had common themes, based on the design and technology of the era. Despite their 30,000 to 40,000 capacities, they were more often cramped than not, with plenty of obstructed seats due to poles supporting upper decks that were in some cases added years into their operation. The close quarters promoted a certain aroma, especially where outfield stands in effect enclosed the ballpark and held in the olfactory prompts of the era, ranging from cigarette smoke early on to marijuana in the 1970s.

With several exceptions, the predominant field dimensions favored the Babe Ruth–prompted style of slugging that came into play in the stadiums' early years. The ballparks were built close to the center of cities, the largest structures of residential or industrial areas that frequently deteriorated as the post-World War II years commenced. But in their prime, they brought all kinds of ethnic groups together in the commonality of baseball.

Getting ready for another game, a renovated Fenway Park
proudly displays Red Sox team colors amid its cozy dimensions.

The ballparks were game changers with their capacities, permitting season attendances of 1 million or more for the first time in their respective franchises' histories.

Philadelphia's Shibe Park, later renamed Connie Mack Stadium, and Pittsburgh's Forbes Field kicked off the building boom in 1909. Chicago's Comiskey Park, hailed as a wondrous

Genevieve Ebbets, youngest daughter of Charley Ebbets, throwing out the first ball at the opening of Ebbets Field on April 5, 1913

structure, began operation in 1910, followed by Washington's Griffith Stadium a year later. Detroit's Navin Field (later evolving into Briggs Stadium and Tiger Stadium), Cincinnati's Crosley Field, and Fenway threw open their doors in 1912. Redone versions of New York's Polo Grounds and St. Louis's Sportsman's Park—renamed Busch Stadium in 1953—also opened in 1912. The sainted Ebbets Field was dedicated in 1913 and Wrigley Field made its debut for the old Federal League Chicago Whales in 1914, then welcomed the Cubs for a century-long-plus stay in 1916. Shibe Park and Sportsman's Park got heavy summer workouts hosting two teams each through the early 1950s.

The architects had more work expanding these early models to gargantuan sizes in the 1920s. Babe Ruth literally helped build Yankee Stadium, opening two years after his 54- and 59-homer seasons in 1920-21 made him New York's top entertainment draw. Nearly a decade later, Cleveland Stadium went into part-time operation hosting the Indians. Both ballparks could accommodate more than 75,000 fans. Meanwhile, a much smaller Municipal Stadium in Kansas City served the Negro League Monarchs until the Athletics moved from Philadelphia in 1955.

Distinctive features and the surrounding environment made most of the ballparks memorable. Fenway became known for its imposing 37-foot-high Green Monster wall. After 1937, Wrigley Field was renowned for its bucolic ivy on the outfield walls and iconic center field scoreboard. Since the first day of the ballpark operation perhaps the most unpredictable features were the winds that turn the structure on the corner of Clark and Addison into two distinctive ballparks depending on the gales' direction. Comiskey Park hosted baseball's first exploding scoreboard. Players took aim to win a suit by hitting the Abe Stark sign on the right field wall at Ebbets Field. Tiger Stadium was renowned for its right field upper-deck overhang, atop which Reggie Jackson hit a transformer with a Ruth-ian clout during the 1971 All-Star Game.

Owners tried to manipulate the dimensions of several of the ballparks to promote power. When Hank Greenberg arrived in Pittsburgh for his final season in 1947, management shortened the porch in left. Nicknamed "Greenberg Gardens," the new area stayed in place for Ralph Kiner's slugging prime. In 1949, White Sox manager Frank Lane shortened the left field dimensions at Comiskey Park, then moved them back the night before the muscle-bound Yankees came in. The American League then prohibited the changing of dimensions mid-season.

When Hank Greenberg arrived in Pittsburgh for his final season in 1947, management shortened the porch in left.

Over the years, the ballparks took plenty of abuse. A fire early in 1934 forced quick reconstruction of parts of Fenway Park. In 1937, 21 feet of water covered Crosley Field. And in 1979, some 70,000 fans nearly shook apart Comiskey Park, with many of that "Disco Demolition" bunch tearing up the sod during a doubleheader.

The modernists took aim at Fenway Park, but owner John Henry's mid-2000s renovation quieted the attempt to replace the icon. Falling concrete from the upper deck in 2004 at Wrigley Field signaled the need for a complete renovation, but work did not really commence for another decade. Wrigley had a kinder fate than Comiskey Park, eight miles south. P. K. Wrigley typically spent a few hundred thousand dollars every offseason on maintenance, extending the ballpark's life in spite of the concrete chunks fiasco. But successive White Sox ownerships could not even afford coffee money for maintenance, and Charles Comiskey's pride and joy slowly crumbled until a threat to move the team in 1988 forced Illinois to approve the building of what is now U.S. Cellular Field.

Fenway and Wrigley proudly still stand and will host the Red Sox and Cubs into the foreseeable future. Hints of their ballpark contemporaries and their own best features were incorporated into the wave of new ballparks, such as oddball dimensions, short porches to accommodate sluggers, and a sloped hill in center field in Houston's Minute Maid Park.

NFL and college teams used to shoehorn their fields into the baseball-oriented old ballparks. Then, the multipurpose stadiums more favored their football tenants at the expense of baseball. Now, fittingly, when Wrigley hosted a Northwestern-Illinois football game in 2010, the football field could no longer be squeezed into a a north-south layout as in the 50 seasons the Bears played there due to seating additions over the decades. But in the new east-west alignment, not enough room was left in the east end zone for a receiver to run full speed out of bounds without racking himself up on the brick wall. Both teams had to run their offenses in the opposite direction, aiming for the west end zone that had foul territory beyond it as slack. The ballpark was designed for baseball.

Throwback Ballparks
New Digs Bring Money, Circuses, Tradition to the Game

NO. **41**

Start out with a spacious design, but keep overall capacity to around 40,000 to maintain ticket scarcity. Locate in or near a city's downtown. Carve out some quirky dimensions like a short home-run porch in left or right field, or an upper-deck overhang. Incorporate the surrounding cityscape into the layout, including using an actual building as a left field perch. Dramatically expand the menu from the traditional hot dogs, peanuts, and Cracker Jack.

The designers have gotten it right more often than not in the third ballpark building boom of the past 100 years. They incorporated the best features of the first wave circa 1910, and took care to avoid the numbing mistakes of the multipurpose cookie-cutter stadiums that stained the game from the mid-1960s to the mid-1970s.

The only drawbacks are overall higher ticket prices, as baseball has evolved somewhat from its longtime status as the most economical and accessible sport for budget-minded fans. Amid the building of the new ballparks, the average fan simply cannot wake up one morning and impulsively decide to take the family to a game. Upper decks featuring the most affordable tickets are sometimes in the nosebleed regions due to the need to stack luxury suites in between the lower and upper seating areas. Steep inclines in the slope of the upper deck induce acrophobia for some fans. Where are the decent, affordable seats?

The way-in-advance forerunners of the new wave were built in Los Angeles and Kansas City. Dodger Stadium, opened in 1962, was the first of the modern ballparks built without posts in the lower deck that obstructed sightlines of the field. Clean and spacious with a

Oriole Park at Camden Yards was the first—and many say the best—of the new wave of ballparks with retro features.

56,000 capacity, Walter O'Malley's field of dreams has stood the test of time with some handy renovations. However, it offered a harbinger of the future with an upper deck that was the equivalent of nine stories above the field with the players reduced to tiny faraway figures.

Southern California got its second new ballpark of the decade when Anaheim Stadium, now Angels Stadium, opened in 1966. The Angels needed their own home after starting out in the minor-league Wrigley Field in Los Angeles in 1961, then sharing Dodger Stadium with their NL landlords for four seasons starting in 1962. The multipurpose stadiums then began proliferating until the beautiful Kauffman Stadium replaced creaky Municipal Stadium in Kansas City in 1973. Totally open-air, the park originally called Royals Stadium established the later standard of topping out at around 40,000 capacity. Distinctive fountains highlighted the outfield backdrop. The ballpark was updated during the recent stadium building boom with more seating along with party and special-events areas in the outfield.

By the late 1980s, HOK Sports Facilities Group, the leading ballpark architectural firm, had concepts for the present wave of stadiums with distinctive, quirky features. The first design implemented, though, was Chicago's new Comiskey Park in 1991, later renamed U.S. Cellular Field. Reportedly, the Illinois Sports Facilities Authority and the tenant White Sox had the option of building a new-age structure that was in the HOK blueprints, but instead opted for the old Kauffman Stadium–style design.

The model for most ballparks to follow was finally locked in via Oriole Park at Camden Yards in Baltimore. Seats close to the action, cozy home-run distances, the design's incorporation of the B & O Warehouse beyond right field, the conversion of Eutaw Street adjoining the warehouse into a walkway with concession stands, and the view of downtown Baltimore beyond

On Attracting Fans to Baseball Games

"If the people don't want to come out to the ballpark, nobody's going to stop them." —*Yogi Berra*

SPITBALLING

center field became standard features for numerous ballparks to come. Camden Yards played a key role in the revival of interest following the devastating 1994-95 strike. On September 6, 1995, Cal Ripken Jr. broke Lou Gehrig's ironman record by playing in his 2,131st game amid the hoopla in a nationally telecast affair via ESPN. Over the next decade, Camden Yards was joined by several new ballparks that stuck out from the rest of the pack for their quality. AT&T Park in San Francisco ended the fans' chilled inconvenience watching games at wind-swept Candlestick Park. Cozy seating and the incorporation of the McCovey Cove inlet, in which kayakers staked out in hopes of snaring a dunked home-run ball, were prime attractions.

More than 2,000 miles to the east, owner Kevin McClatchy insisted his Pirates needed a new ballpark in order to make a go of it in Pittsburgh. So the well-rated PNC Park opened in 2001, complete with scenic views of downtown Pittsburgh and a San Francisco right field replica via the Allegheny River as destination for a well-clouted ball. The Roberto Clemente Bridge beyond center field carried pedestrians from downtown. But the Pirates continued to wallow in the National League's netherworld despite the financial and aesthetic boost from the stadium. Finally, beauty matched opportunity when the right management team enabled the Buccos to rise to contender's status in 2013. Build it—a good team—and they will come, when paired with an attractive stadium. Fans who were slow to patronize Three Rivers Stadium despite some great "Lumber Company" teams and Hall of Famers now pack PNC Park with franchise-record season attendances.

Fans who were slow to patronize Three Rivers Stadium despite some great "Lumber Company" teams and Hall of Famers now pack PNC Park with franchise-record season attendances.

Other praised ballparks in the new wave and their opening dates included Progessive Field in Cleveland (1994), Safeco Field in Seattle (1999), Comerica Park in Detroit (2000), Miller Park in Milwaukee (2001), Petco Park in San Diego (2004) and Target Field in Minneapolis (2010). New York opened a grander replacement for Yankee Stadium and Citi Field supplanted Shea Stadium, both in 2009. A third version of Busch Stadium opened in St. Louis in 2006 with a "Ballpark Village" with bread and circuses on the old ballpark footprint.

Designers copied the Wrigley Field rooftop experiences just outside Busch Stadium, atop a building beyond Minute Maid Park's left field wall and on the roof of the four-story Western Metal Supply Co. building, incorporated down the left field line into Petco Park's layout. Meanwhile, the left field Crawford Boxes, just 315 feet from home plate at Minute Maid Park, is one of the most popular short porches in the wave of new parks.

Despite costlier tickets, new parks changed baseball's attendance game.

William L. Veeck

The First, Less Colorful Veeck Has Most Long-Term Impact in the Family

NO. **42**

Whereas no photo seems to exist of Bill Veeck, nicknamed "Sport Shirt Bill," wearing a tie, all old images of father William L. Veeck show a dignified man wearing a high, tight collar of the fashion of Herbert Hoover and the 1920s. Most often the elder Veeck was fitted into a double-breasted suit. He was outfitted in the duds of command, establishment, and convention.

The first Veeck in baseball was anything but a man of convention. And that's why even though his legacy can by overshadowed by that of his far-better-known son, a Hall of Famer nicknamed the "Baseball Barnum," William L. Veeck had more impact in the long run than his bread-and-circuses offspring. And if the truth be known, the colorful ways in which Bill Veeck turned baseball on its ear had their basis in his father's philosophies. To the end of his life, Bill Veeck revered the memory of his father, calling him "Daddy." A quick summary of the elder Veeck's accomplishments as president of a Chicago Cubs franchise he turned into an economic hyper-power by the end of the 1920s backs up the higher rating than his son's. How about extensive radio coverage of baseball? Move on to season tickets, tickets sold at a location other than the ballpark, and the inclusion of women as fans through wildly popular Ladies Days that turned them into paying customers.

Veeck triggered the grand jury investigation that led to the Black Sox Scandal. Amid the gambling quagmire, he was a big advocate for Kenesaw Mountain Landis's ascension as

William L. Veeck and assistant Margaret Donahue look over ticket orders for the 1929 World Series.

the game's first commissioner to bring order to baseball. Later, he pushed for the first All-Star Game and advocated interleague play.

Even before he began building a team that would be as powerful, albeit briefly, as the Babe Ruth–led New York Yankees, former sportswriter Veeck had an impact on the game. In 1920, he was involved in two incidents that cracked down on the incipient gambling and potential game-fixing that had bedeviled baseball in that era. The second of the events involved six anonymous telegrams and two phone calls warning Veeck that the day's game with the Philadelphia Phillies would be fixed. Four suspected Cubs were left off the traveling roster for the road trip. A Cook County grand jury was soon impaneled to investigate gambling in baseball, but quickly switched from the attempted Cubs fix to long-percolating rumors the White Sox had fixed the 1919 World Series against the Cincinnati Reds.

Five years later, Veeck green-lighted radio coverage of the Cubs. Fledgling radio stations broadcast as many games as possible without being charged a rights fee. Veeck found out cars parked near Wrigley Field bore the license plates of five surrounding states thanks to the broadcasts. Radio was credited with the Cubs setting the major-league attendance record of nearly 1.5 million in 1929. By 1931, as many as seven stations simultaneously broadcast the Cubs. Meanwhile, other key owners, including those of all three New York–area teams, restricted or banned broadcasts for fear they would cut into the gate. The process worked exactly the opposite, as the moguls eventually discovered. Philip Wrigley—in one of his few good ownership tactics—mimicked the open-door broadcast policy when television came on the scene in the late 1940s.

Meanwhile, Veeck and his one-time stenographer Margaret Donahue, to whom he gave management responsibilities as baseball's pioneering female executive, changed the nature of baseball crowds. Formerly a bastion of smoky, cigar-chomping testosterone, the Veeck-led Cubs prompted an invasion of women via the free Ladies Days. The influx of female fans was so enthusiastic they spilled into the outfield, where they stood by the thousands

SHORT LIST

William L. Veeck's Top Five Achievements

Built the last long-term Chicago Cubs contender, lasting from 1927 to 1939.

Allowed widespread radio coverage of the Cubs, setting the stage for the broadcast industry's long-term relationship with baseball.

Boosted women's interest in baseball with wildly popular Ladies Days.

Took stand against attempted game-fixing that led to the investigation of the Black Sox Scandal.

Backed innovations like the All-Star Game and interleague play.

behind ropes. Balls hit into the crowd were ground-rule doubles. The women overwhelmed the turnstiles with a Ladies Day total gates peaking between 45,000 and 51,000 in 1929 and 1930. Of course, the main attraction in this boom in baseball business was the Cubs themselves. Under Veeck, the team acquired Hack Wilson, Gabby Hartnett, Kiki Cuyler, Charlie Grimm, Riggs Stephenson, Woody English, Charlie Root, and other key contributors to a powerful team that was likened to the Yankees. Later Veeck acquisitions included infielders Billy Herman and Billy Jurges. The team did not win any of the four World Series in which they played through 1938, but ranked with the New York Giants and St. Louis Cardinals as a consistent contender through that period.

Formerly a bastion of smoky, cigar-chomping testosterone, the Veeck-led Cubs prompted an invasion of women via the free Ladies Days.

William Veeck also was a big backer of the first All-Star Game, held in conjunction with the Century of Progress world's fair in Chicago in 1933. Around the same time, he also advocated interleague play as a fix to the plummeting attendance besetting baseball in the depths of the Great Depression.

"I go to baseball meetings, but nobody suggests how we can get more patrons into our parks," Veeck told the *Sporting News*' Harry Neily in 1933. "I am not certain what can be done, but we are conducting our business on the basis of two decades ago.

"Every other line of endeavor has changed its tactics, but we go along in the same old rut . . . baseball cannot stand still and survive."

Good or bad economy, the Cubs likely would have continued as a winning franchise under Veeck, who had shown his ability to build powerhouse teams player by player. When Philip K. Wrigley succeeded his father as owner early in 1932, he basically gave Veeck ownership authority on his behalf. But Veeck's death at the end of the 1933 season from a fast-spreading leukemia threw leadership of the team up for grabs. Within two years, Wrigley named himself team president for want of finding "another Bill Veeck." The shy mogul simply could not hire anyone as capable and creative as his late president, and the stage was set for the Cubs' record-long championship drought.

Wrigley then employed a series of sycophants and incompetents to run the team while he meddled to disastrous results. Executives of successor owner Tribune Company caught the meddling disease themselves in the 1980s, further lengthening the Cubs' long, strange journey.

All the results are in black and white. William L. Veeck's life—and death—was a huge game changer for baseball in general (and the Cubs in particular).

Bill Veeck
Bringing the Circus to Town

An outcast, even a pariah, for much of his big-league career in the eyes of traditional own- ers, "Barnum Bill" Veeck thought of a baseball game as one part of an all-inclusive enter- tainment package. Nine innings of ballplaying action, to be sure—and more before the first pitch, in the stands, and on the borders of the ballpark. Even dropping from the sky, as when "Martians" alighted from a helicopter to "kidnap" Nellie Fox and Luis Aparicio.

NO. 43

A second-generation baseball executive, Veeck went beyond the conventional "church of baseball" thinking and saw the game as entertainment. He brought light times and laughs through an exploding scoreboard, a 3'7" batter, fans voting on strategy via signs in the grandstands, and a seventh-inning singalong by an off- key announcer. Anything that makes the day or night memorable—even a "disco demolition" promotion that goes horribly wrong.

What Veeck wrought out of his fertile mind is now standard operating procedure throughout baseball. The game is not enough. Bread and circuses are part of the ticket price.

No matter how many knocks he took, the lords of the realm could not rip his pedigree. He was the son of the respected Cubs president William L. Veeck, whose lasting innovations paved the way for his son. As a young Cubs official in 1937, four years after his father's premature death, the younger Veeck supervised the installation of Wrigley Field's celebrated bleachers, manual center field scoreboard, and trademark ivy. He had conceived the idea of the ivy as far back as age 13.

A man with a social conscience who had even greater empathy for others after losing part of his left leg to the recoil of a gun as a World War II Marine, Veeck signed the first African-American player in the American League three months after Jackie Robinson's 1947 debut for the Brooklyn Dodgers. Cleveland Indians outfielder Larry Doby ended up a

A bare-chested Bill Veeck is in his element in Wrigley Field's center field bleachers in 1981 as he talks to the author.

trailblazer twice for Veeck. Thirty-one years later, he became the major leagues' second black manager for Veeck's White Sox.

Selling the Indians after the breakup of his first marriage and moving on to St. Louis, Veeck's promotional acumen really took off in 1951. The usually bad "Brownies" really needed a distraction from their poor play. The owner, literally living in Sportsman's Park with new wife Mary Frances Veeck, outfoxed the American League to sign Eddie Gaedel, an entertainer afflicted with dwarfism, to bat one time on August 19, 1951. Veeck also had a grandstand manager's day in which the fans voted on strategy for the Browns.

American League owners, angry at the maverick Veeck, prevented him from moving the Browns to Baltimore, then executed a double-whammy, forcing him to sell the team to ownership that was then allowed to move to Maryland.

After working as a consultant for old boss Philip K. Wrigley, Veeck came back to buy Dorothy Rigney Comiskey's majority share of the White Sox in 1959. Veeck unveiled his pièce de résistance early in 1960—baseball's first exploding scoreboard, the pyrotechnics set up to celebrate each Sox homer. Visitors mocked the huge contraption. The Yankees set off sparklers by their dugout. Certifiably nuts outfielder Jimmy Piersall threw a ball at the scoreboard. But noisy home-team celebrations were here to stay.

Veeck's first stay as White Sox owner was not long. He sold his shares to partner Arthur Allyn Jr., ostensibly due to health problems, in mid-season 1961. Veeck decamped to Maryland's Eastern Shore for the next 14 years, operating the Suffolk Downs racetrack while syndicating a newspaper column, TV show, and radio commentaries. Like a character out of a novel, Veeck made a triumphant return to Chicago late in 1975. He was the bail-out purchaser

On Little Batters

"Were it in my power to turn back the clock, I'd never send a midget to bat. No, I'd use nine of the little fellows, including the designated hitter." —*Bill Veeck*

SPITBALLING

of the nearly bankrupt White Sox, who were nearly ticketed to be moved to Seattle to assuage that city's anger over losing the expansion Pilots to Milwaukee five years earlier. Again, the AL owners made life difficult for Veeck, voting down his first bid to buy the Sox on the grounds that it was not properly capitalized. Longtime Chicago baseball announcer Jack Brickhouse came to the rescue, helping line up more investors.

Veeck unleashed a new wave of promotions at aging Comiskey Park. He also introduced softball-like uniforms, including shorts that actually were worn for just three games in 1976. The next season, the cash-short owner "rented" free-agent-to-be sluggers Richie Zisk and Oscar

Veeck unleashed a new wave of promotions at aging Comiskey Park.

Gamble for a memorable "South Side Hit Men" season. At the same time, he came up with a truly genius promotion. Veeck spotted broadcaster Harry Caray singing "Take Me Out to the Ballgame" during the seventh-inning stretch. He then learned radio station WMAQ had a tape of Caray's rendition. Veeck asked Caray if he could sing live to the entire crowd. At first Caray refused, but eventually bowed to Veeck's wishes. He sang in his broadcast booth as he wielded his mic like a conductor's baton. The crowd went wild, heartily singing along. A tradition was born, and simply got bigger in spades, popularized on superstation WGN-TV, when Caray moved eight miles north to the Cubs in 1982.

The coup de grace was Disco Demolition Night on July 12, 1979, at Comiskey Park. Mike Veeck, son of the owner and Sox promotions director, got his father to sign off on the idea to have popular disc jockey Steve Dahl blow up disco records between games of a doubleheader with the Detroit Tigers. The promotion worked *too* well. The ol' ballpark was transformed into a rock-concert atmosphere with as many as 70,000 squeezed in and up to 35,000 more clamoring to get in. When Dahl blew up the records, thousands more discs went sailing onto the field, followed by thousands of fans in a joyous riot. Bill Veeck's appeal to clear the field went unheeded. The second game was forfeited to the Tigers. Several weeks later, as "Sodfather" groundskeeper Roger Bossard tried to repair the torn-up field, he found "nine or 10" places where little marijuana plants had sprouted thanks to the impromptu seeding by Disco Demolition merrymakers.

Overwhelmed by baseball's rising economics, Veeck sold the Sox after the 1980 season and retired to the Wrigley center field bleachers he had helped build 43 years previously. Proudly sitting bare-shirted like his fellow bleacher bums and using his peg leg as an ashtray, Veeck paid the $3 admission rather than use his lifetime major-league pass so he could ethically continue to speak his mind. When he died of cancer at 71 in 1986, he had lived two or three lifetimes in one, having shaken up baseball time and again from its comfort zone.

The 1975 World Series

A Shot in the Arm Thanks to Fisk's Shot in the Dark

The 1975 World Series pitted the "Big Red Machine" of Cincinnati, a team many say was the greatest in history, against the upstart Boston Red Sox, stocked with six appealing homegrown players in their lineup. Baseball had been tinkering for six previous years to try to bring back fans and boost offense. But put dramatics into a World Series, stock it with four one-run games, concoct a half dozen memorable scenarios climaxed by a wee-hours walk-off homer in one unforgettable Game 6, and play it all the way down to the ninth inning of Game 7—the 1975 Series gave the game a badly needed shot in the arm. Baseball built it, and the fans came for years afterward.

No one can forget the NBC reaction shot from a camera inside Fenway Park's Green Monster of Carlton Fisk waving and contorting his foul-line hugging drive to stay inches within fair territory. The baseball gods answered Fisk, and the pure joy gave the impression that the Red Sox won the whole thing. But all the Fisk blast at 12:43 a.m. Eastern Time did was book a Game 7 the next night. Some 62 million had watched Game 6 on NBC. Game 7 drew a record 76 million. The majority would become both TV viewers and ticket buyers as baseball enjoyed boom times the remainder of the 1970s and well into another decade.

Baseball moguls had tried a series of moves to reverse pro football's rapid encroachment on the game's pre-eminence. They lowered the mound, tightened the strike zone, and instituted the designated hitter to mixed results on the field and at the gate.

Carlton Fisk begins using his famous body English to wave his game-winning homer fair in the 12th inning of Game 6 of the 1975 World Series at Fenway Park.

"Looking back on it, the Series itself really just put baseball back on the map. Football was kind of becoming America's sport," said 1975 American League MVP Fred Lynn, one of the rare birds who won that top award alongside capturing Rookie of the Year honors as Red Sox center fielder. The Reds had three future Hall of Famers—Johnny Bench, Joe Morgan, Tony Perez—in the batting order, managed by the Cooperstown-bound Sparky Anderson. Include Pete Rose as a Hall of Fame–worthy player if you write off a certain gambling technicality. Meanwhile, the Red Sox fielded homegrown products like Lynn, catcher Fisk, left fielder Jim Rice, right fielder Dwight Evans, shortstop Rick Burleson, and first baseman Cecil Cooper.

The series was tied 2–2 with three one-run games. Game 3 in Riverfront Stadium was decided in the bottom of the 10th by a controversial non-interference call on Reds pinch hitter Ed Armbrister. Fisk thought Armbrister interfered with him when the latter tried to bunt, and forced a bad throw to second trying to nab Cesar Geronimo. Umpire Larry Barnett refused to call interference, giving the Reds enough impetus to win moments later.

The Red Sox were backed to their own left field wall coming back to Fenway down 3–2 for a Game 6 pushed back three days from a Saturday to Tuesday by rain. Lynn slugged a three-run homer in the first, then the Reds tied the game in the fifth. Three innings later, the Reds had a 6–3 lead. Ex-Red Bernie Carbo, pinch hitting in the eighth, barely fought off a tough pitch from Cincy closer Rawly Eastwick before belting a game-tying homer to center that would have been an all-time classic if there hadn't been more theatrics in store.

The Red Sox were primed to win in the bottom of the ninth, but the Reds' George Foster rifled a throw from a tough angle down the left field line after catching a short fly to cut down Denny Doyle at the plate. Doyle thought he heard third base coach Don Zimmer yelling, "Go! Go! Go!" when Zimmer really said, "No! No! No!" Then Boston returned the favor in the bottom of the 11th. Morgan lofted a long fly toward Pesky's Pole in the right field corner, at first glance a go-ahead homer. But a sprinting Evans snared the ball before it dipped over the fence, whirled and doubled Ken Griffey Sr. off first.

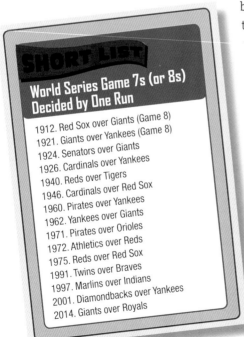

SHORT LIST

World Series Game 7s (or 8s) Decided by One Run

1912. Red Sox over Giants (Game 8)
1921. Giants over Yankees (Game 8)
1924. Senators over Giants
1926. Cardinals over Yankees
1940. Reds over Tigers
1946. Cardinals over Red Sox
1960. Pirates over Yankees
1962. Yankees over Giants
1971. Pirates over Orioles
1972. Athletics over Reds
1975. Reds over Red Sox
1991. Twins over Braves
1997. Marlins over Indians
2001. Diamondbacks over Yankees
2014. Giants over Royals

Leading off the bottom of the 12th as viewers in the East and Midwest time zones fought off sleep was Fisk. The recording of one of sports' all-time greatest images was a result of the collaboration of NBC camera operator Lou Gerard and a rat inside the Green Monster.

Gerard's assignment from pre-eminent baseball director Harry Coyle was first to follow the ball and, if that was not possible, get Fisk's reaction. The misty night forced Gerard to focus on Fisk. But then he noticed the big rodent just four feet away.

"The rat helped make the shot," Coyle told baseball broadcasting biographer Curt Smith in his seminal *Voices of the Game* book. "See, Lou had one eye on the rat and one on the camera—he was preoccupied, you can imagine—so when Fisk hit the ball, Gerard didn't dare go through the movement needed to shift the viewfinder and follow the ball. He played it nice and safe and stationary—he kept the lens on Fisk. Who knows, if the rat hadn't shown up for a guest appearance, it's possible Lou would have switched to the ball, even with the mist. And we'd have missed the shot which really changed TV sports coverage around [close-ups focusing on athletes' reactions]."

The recording of one of sports' all-time greatest images was a result of the collaboration of NBC camera operator Lou Gerard and a rat inside the Green Monster.

Recalled Lynn: "The commissioner of baseball was there, everybody who was anybody was there at those last two games at Fenway Park. It was a little bit of David vs. Goliath, but we already slew Goliath in the Oakland A's. There was so much going on, and so many good players involved and so many exciting things happening. It was just tons of excitement, tons of drama."

The quota of drama every inning quieted down for Game 7, which of course was decided by one run. The Boston cynics had a field day watching the Red Sox unable to hold a 3–0 first-inning lead, eventually yielding on Morgan's parachute single to center off southpaw Jim Burton in the top of the ninth.

Baseball got its shot in the arm and enjoyed boom times over the next decade. Attendance increased by 50 percent in the decade from 1976 forward, while revenues tripled. The Reds affirmed their place in history, while Red Sox Nation was established for the long run as the team garnered a win despite the World Series loss on paper.

The Red Sox finished out of the money in the following season. But it didn't matter in the long run. The 1975 World Series stuck to the emotional ribs in Boston, Cincinnati, and so many points far beyond.

Interleague Play

Settling Arguments That Could Never Before Be Settled on the Field

Resolution, finally. My-team-is-better-than-yours debates could finally be settled in box scores via interleague play starting in 1997.

Part of a series of competitive innovations like the wild card and division series, interleague play was particularly welcomed in two-team markets like New York, Chicago, Los Angeles, and the San Francisco Bay Area. Fans in one-team towns who never saw stars in the other league in person now had a chance to watch some of that complement visit annually.

The question is now, after two full decades of interleague play, whether the original attraction has worn off, since the initial novelty has long passed. Is interleague play, now scheduled regularly throughout the season rather than segregated into a specific time frame, now nothing more special than any other game? Has it dulled the old American League–National League rivalries that used to play out only in the All-Star Game and the World Series? Is interleague play the leading edge of a homogenization of baseball in which there are no league offices, the umpiring crews are co-mingled, and the only real structural difference is the DH in the AL?

Baseball beauty—or lack thereof—is in the eye of the beholder. Cynics and scolds will rip the interleague system as they'd nitpick any other aspect of baseball. A decidedly positive view seems to be connected to whether the two-team cities, which generate a lot of media opinion due to sheer market size, feature winning teams with the competitive juices

In laid-back Southern California, Dodgers and Angels fans could show their colors without conflict when their teams played each other.

flowing even more for interleague action. Two losing teams facing off in one city six times only compound the collective misery about town, and thus prompt calls for changes in the system.

Interleague play had been proposed for much of the 20th century. Advocates seemed to concentrate in the two-team markets, where exhibition games between the teams were popular annual events, given the rarity of inter-city World Series after the Dodgers and Giants had fled to the West Coast late in 1957. In the interleague era, the Yankees and Mets, and Giants and Athletics have played each other in the World Series just one time apiece.

Interleague contests enabled Dodgers and Angels players to renew old acquaintances before the game.

The Mets and Yankees played each other annually in a mid-season game in New York. Howie "Disco Schloss" Schlossberg, a future editor and journalism professor, had a good vantage point as a hot dog vendor at the inter-city rivalry game at Shea Stadium in 1968.

"Biggest crowd was Mets-Yankees Mayor's Cup game, an exhibition then," Schlossberg said. "Ah, the Mets and Yankees—so far ahead of their time. No bringing up minor leaguers to play this one. Blood and pride on the line. Seaver and Koosman were available. Just in case. All hands on deck for this exhibition."

The Cubs and White Sox played a similar mid-season game in Chicago—the Boys Benefit Game, raising money for youth programs. Crowds swelled to as many as 52,000—several thousand more than capacity—for the 1964 edition at night at Comiskey Park. A Thursday afternoon game featuring Burt Hooton's big-league pitching debut at Wrigley Field in 1971 drew a near-capacity 34,000. Hall of Famer Ernie Banks took his last-ever swings in an exhibition game in the Boys Benefit contest in 1972 at Comiskey, nearly a year after his final regular season at-bat.

Nearly 2,000 miles to the west, the Dodgers and Angels staged their annual three-game Freeway Series in Los Angeles and Anaheim to conclude spring training. "I played for the Angels in the Dodgers' heyday, when they had [Steve] Garvey, [Ron] Cey, [Davey] Lopes, and we had Reggie [Jackson], Don Baylor, Bobby Grich," said former star center fielder Fred Lynn. "They had 55,000 in LA and we had 63,000 in Anaheim [with extra capacity] because the

Rams played there then. Those were big gates. It was bragging rights for the town. It felt like a real game. It was spring training, but it didn't feel like it with 63,000. We played hard. It was no-holds-barred, believe me."

Eventually, such intensity was allowed to manifest itself for real when the interleague schedule was introduced. Like any newfangled thing, the games that matched natural geographical rivalries were raucous affairs for the fans with often playoff intensity on the field. A Michael Barrett vs. A.J. Pierzynski one-round bout at home plate at U.S. Cellular Field in 2006 seemed the peak of the fiery atmosphere. But after a decade, some of the sheer emotion started to fade. Veteran columnist Bernie Lincicome, a bearer of sarcasm and cynicism in healthy doses, had his first-string rapier out for interleague games in his weekly *Chicago Tribune* column on July 12, 2005:

"Interleague play has always been a phony novelty, a cynical gimmick to try to dupe the public into the ballpark, and has nothing to do with baseball's essence, its charm or which is the best team in the league. It tarnishes what is distinctive about baseball in exchange for the brief and the cheap.

"Baseball does not boast of the quality of interleague play, it boasts of the increased attendance, or it frets when attendance does not rise to the bait."

Far more thoughtful than cynical was New York Mets outfielder Curtis Granderson, who suggested all 30 teams should play each other one series a season, rather than alternating and having each AL division play a different NL division each year with only certain crosstown and geographic rivalries occurring annually. "From a fan's standpoint, I'd really love to see the opposition come in once, if not every year, than at least every other year," Granderson told the *Chicago Tribune* in 2015.

Like any newfangled thing, the games that matched natural geographical rivalries were raucous affairs.

Interleague play may have gone stale in some places. Yet in one corner of the country, home to plenty of transplanted fans, it is eagerly anticipated.

"We live in the San Diego area, and if the Yankees, the Red Sox or the Orioles come play here, it's a big deal. You can't get a ticket," said Lynn.

"These are the [AL] Eastern clubs the Padres would never see unless they get into the World Series. It's a big deal to see these guys come into town. You're still going to get some games where they say, 'Who cares?' But there are a lot of games where a lot of people do care. It creates a lot of buzz where there may not be. If the Padres are scuffling and the Yankees come to town, there are three games that will sell out."

1:45:49PM

comcast SPORTSNET

Superstations and Regional Sports Networks
Cabling Up the Game

A little-watched Atlanta UHF station, one step away from bankruptcy, launched a baseball-viewing revolution that shifted games from the over-the-air outlets to first a handful of superstations, then regional sports networks for almost every team. Billions of dollars were infused into baseball's coffers. But when the rights fees become so large that cable carriers are finally unable to pass along the charges to subscribers, the electronic spigot is turned off. Such is the case with the Los Angeles Dodgers' ill-advised grab for gold with Time Warner Cable, in which some 70 percent of the team's home market could not receive the new regional sports network's games because area cable carriers were unwilling to charge $5 a subscriber to offset the fees TWC had demanded.

"I don't think we've reached a ceiling because the value of sports shows itself time and time again," said Phil Bedella, general manager of Comcast SportsNet Chicago. "The launch of the SEC Network, the launch of the Longhorn Network, you see all these things happening.

"There's more challenges because of [the quest for] profits. It probably makes it harder for one-team regionals. But sports is so powerful and so important. You see it every day. Sports is one of the few things people will watch live. They're not taping it to their DVR and watching it three days later. They're watching it live. To have that kind of programming on your air, it is a must-have."

Comcast SportsNet Chicago's remote truck is typical of the many-angled baseball production for today's regional sports networks.

For three decades since the first widespread baseball TV deals in the late 1940s, fans took what their screens gave them.

For three decades since the first widespread baseball TV deals in the late 1940s, fans took what their screens gave them. If they lived within signal reach of New York and Chicago over-the-air stations, they enjoyed up to several hundred games per year. But the majority of big-league markets offered half or less of the full schedule as owners worried about home-game telecasts hurting their gate. Large tracts of the country had to settle for just CBS's and NBC's Games of the Week (in the 1950s and early 1960s), later reduced to just one Saturday game on NBC.

Ted Turner changed all that. Operator of an Atlanta-based billboard company, the voluble Turner bought the money-losing Channel 17, crafting new call letters WTCG ("Watch This Channel Grow"), in 1970. Four years later, he acquired the Braves' TV rights from original home WSB-TV, the huge local NBC affiliate. In the middle of the five-year deal, Turner also bought the bedraggled, unpopular Braves. Meanwhile, Turner began beaming WTCG's signal via satellite all over the Southeast.

Eventually, the channel, later renamed WTBS, was seen across the country—timed exquisitely as cable subscriptions skyrocketed from less than 13 million in 1977 to 24 million in 1982—35 percent of US television households. The Braves were branded "America's Team."

Concurrently, WGN-TV, the Chicago Cubs' longtime flagship, televised up to 150 games per season, by far the most in the majors. WGN "passively" put its signal on the satellite, retaining its Chicago focus and not specifically marketing itself as a superstation. The Cubs' telecasts also earned a nationwide audience thanks to bombastic announcer Harry Caray, and then the team's first championship of any kind in 39 years in 1984 when they won the NL East.

Major League Baseball worried about the mass incursion of the superstations into teams' markets and demanded compensation. But the genie was out of the bottle. By 1989, ESPN was fully vested as a baseball telecast partner and truly came into its own as baseball allowed a year-round major-league presence just a decade into the World Wide Leader's existence.

Mass distribution on basic cable gave rise to the regional sports networks, the model for which snared the majority of two or more franchises' TV schedules while injecting new cash flow into teams. Chuck Dolan began SportsChannel in the New York market, signing up both the Mets and Yankees. Now, a minority of Yankees games were carried on WPIX. As the years progressed, a series of SportsChannel services, then Fox Sports (fill in the blank for the specific region) cropped up nationwide. A really big player muscled in via Comcast in Philadelphia, then Chicago, Boston, and the San Francisco Bay Area. The money flowed into teams. Eventually the Cubs allied themselves with Fox Sports Chicago, reducing the number of games to a minority of the schedule on WGN. The Braves migrated to SportSouth.

The Yankees and Red Sox began their own networks, YES and New England Sports Network (NESN). The era of the superstations was drawing to a close with regional sports networks making baseball a cable game for most non-network national telecasts.

A baseball TV director has no shortage of equipment at his disposal in the remote truck.

Dodgers fans were used to local TV scarcity for their team. When the franchise moved to Los Angeles in 1958, only the 11 games in San Francisco against the arch-rival Giants were televised. The number of Dodgers games did increase when regional sports networks were set up in the closing decade of the 20th century. But that cable road eventually led to the much-ripped Time Warner Cable deal in Los Angeles. Dodgers telecasts drew a big-league worst 0.75 rating at mid-season 2015 due to their unavailability for the majority of the nation's No. 2 video market. Vin Scully, a baseball monument, could only be heard for the first three innings on KABC-Radio for those who could not receive the telecasts. On April 1, 2015, *Los Angeles Times* columnist Bill Plaschke wrote about the plight of Dodgers loyalist Jim Ballard, 94, a World War II veteran and Bronze Star awardee. Ballard's daily fix of watching his team on TV was over.

"I feel so helpless," Ballard told Plaschke. "It's like my team just forgot all about me . . . Screw 'em. The hell with them."

The *New York Post* reported the going rate for Time Warner Cable was more in the range of $3 per subscriber. The potential charge to the cable operator, taking a huge bath, was projected to be nearly $1 billion. With only the Dodgers on its roster of teams as an audience lure, the miscalculation of the financial threshold of both cable-carrier and viewer was huge.

Will baseball become a studio game, with fans opting for their huge HD screens at home or the tiny images on the hand-helds in place of the ballpark experience?

"I still think there is an emotion, and just a moment in time you can capture when you're at a live sports event that you can't replicate at home," said Comcast Chicago's Bedella. "Yes, the picture is beautiful and you have great views. But that camaraderie of sitting with your family or friend [and seeing athletic accomplishment], that can't be replicated in a house."

The Center Field Camera

A Now Classic View of Baseball

Whoever imagined the viewer at home, staring intently at a 12-inch black and white TV screen, would in the same year share the same view as New York Giants spies who possibly "telescoped" their way into a shocking pennant?

Such was the innovation of 1951. A Giants observer using a magnifying lens to steal signs from the Polo Grounds clubhouse 500 feet away in center may have had a hand in Bobby Thomson's "Shot Heard 'Round The World" and other achievements as the New Yorkers stormed from far behind to overtake the Brooklyn Dodgers. Oddly enough, the home-bound snooper on the pitcher-batter profile enjoyed his breakthrough in a Little League park some 800 miles to the west.

NO. 47

In another of the breakthroughs emblematic of Chicago home-screen power WGN-TV's 68-season baseball coverage history, the standard center field camera shot was invented out of necessity around 1951 at Thillens Stadium, on the Chicago city limits about six miles northwest of Wrigley Field.

Within a few years, the pitcher-batter view—at first thought of as disorienting by some TV execs and downright intrusive by hidebound baseball officials—became the gateway for millions to watch the game. Countless batters' stances and swings along with Sandy Koufax's rising fastballs and Greg Maddux's back-door control pitch that dipped back over the inside corner at the last second to lefty hitters were shown to revealing effect by increasingly more powerful camera lenses. Now, the center field camera stands as the potential final frontier for officially second-guessing balls and strikes.

A typical center field camera shot, from Comcast SportsNet Chicago.
Some networks have multiple center field cameras now.

Filling time in the holes of the Dumont Network's primetime schedule, WGN televised Little League games weekly with announcer Jack Brickhouse during the summer from the quaint Thillens ballpark, owned by a check-cashing firm. But the crew had one problem. The tiny stands behind the plate had no room for a camera to frame the pitcher, batter, and umpire in one shot, the standard baseball coverage shot in early TV. The WGN crew had to find an alternative.

A 1953 listing for the primetime Little League telecast, helmed by Jack Brickhouse, on which the center field camera was tried before major-league use

Then-director Jack Jacobson and a "framer" walked around Thillens and found a shot that worked, in center field. Another factor also came into play—the camera could only be placed as far as cable could be strung.

"You go to a ballpark, you find a place to park your truck and you've got to run all this cable," said Bill Lotzer, who began directing WGN's baseball games in 1954. Good fortune found the parking lot in which WGN's control truck was stationed just beyond the right field fence.

"The distance from the truck to that position was shorter than to other positions," Lotzer, 88 in 2015, recalled. "You have to bear on the fact the camera cables in those days were quite big and heavy. You have to string all this cable. They felt that was a better position. It kind of fell in and away we went."

Jacobson recalled—although precise memories might be off—that WGN adopted the center field camera the next day at Wrigley Field.

TV-friendly Cubs owner Philip K. Wrigley okayed the new camera position and slapped on no restrictions. But the telling eye from center did not get such an enthusiastic reception elsewhere.

Yankees' flagship WPIX-TV, like WGN owned by Tribune Company, claimed in an internal company publication that it made first use of the center field camera in a big-league game. But in actuality, the station had two hurdles to its widespread use. WPIX itself believed the Zoomar lens would steal catcher's signals. Meanwhile, Yankees GM George Weiss actually projected himself into 21st-century thought with a feeling that the center field camera angle was so up close and personal that it might discourage attendance. Sign-stealing concerns also were a factor cited by baseball commissioner Ford Frick's temporary ban of the camera in 1959.

But once pioneering network TV director Harry Coyle believed in the shot, the camera would be a staple of NBC coverage. A 25-foot platform was constructed for the camera at County Stadium in Milwaukee for the 1957 World Series. Coyle was able to use the camera as the Milwaukee games were televised in black and white. Fewer giant RCA TK-41 cameras were employed for color telecasts out of Yankee Stadium. None could be spared for the center field shot.

As cable and control-truck technology improved, the center field shot became standard. "The size of the cable diminished," said Lotzer. "When you had a 100-foot roll of [heavy] cable before, you had to do some hauling."

The modern fan watching rerun of a 1950s broadcast would be thrown off by the then-standard shot from behind the plate at near field level. The umpire and catcher appear to get in the way, and the break of pitches cannot easily be discerned.

One baseball controversy could have been settled by the center field camera. The mysterious unavailability of WGN's RCA machine for one batter on September 2, 1972, will leave forever unsettled whether Cubs pitcher Milt Pappas threw a perfect game against the Padres. Pappas had retired the first 26 batters before running the count to 1-and-2 on pinch hitter Larry Stahl. Pappas then threw three pitches called balls by umpire Bruce Froemming. He claimed two of the pitches were strikes. On the previous two Padres batters, director Arne Harris employed the center field camera. But the device was absent for Stahl, and the only broadcast view of the pitches was a high home plate camera that looked down on the backs of Froemming and catcher Randy Hundley. Perhaps Harris was attempting to frame a shot with Pappas's reaction if he got the third strike. But it was logical he would have used the center field shot, as Lotzer had done on final batter Joe Cunningham in Cubs hurler Don Cardwell's 1960 no-hitter. Harris died in 2001, so we cannot get the definitive explanation. Lotzer, WGN's head of producers/directors in 1972, could only speculate that the center field camera had a technical problem at just the wrong time. Pappas had the "consolation" of retiring one more batter to complete a no-hitter, but will caustically pit his word against Froemming's in a never-ending comical duel, without the electronic proof.

Broadcast crews everywhere now use the "pitch tracks" to show where a sequence of pitches crossed the plate area.

Broadcast crews everywhere now use the "pitch tracks" to show where a sequence of pitches crossed the plate area. Umpires are now electronically shown to have missed calls, as they have admitted ever since the game was invented. With replay's foot squarely in the door and video technology continuing to improve by the year, will the Rubicon be crossed to permit replays—and reversals—of balls-and-strikes calls?

Decline of Newspapers
Not Your Father's Sports Section

NO. 48

What was black, white and read all over was once the primary conduit to the daily drama of the long, long season for millions of fans. The game story, originally semi-dry play-by-play accounts, eventually had quotes added when broadcast media grew in competition. Then more content in the daily package: notes, a sidebar, a visit from a columnist, and always, always, the box scores.

The century-long daily paper-reading routine is now up for grabs, and the baseball consuming public is poorer for it. The considerably thinner-yet-more-expensive print copy you might handle isn't your father's newspaper anymore. Changing times, diverted advertisers, and rampaging technology have radically changed consumers' reading habits and destroyed the age-old business model that made newspapers baseball's medium of choice.

It's been a half-century process, dramatically speeded by the dominance of the Internet in a new century. The coup de grace was Craigslist and other online outlets' almost complete hijacking of lucrative classified ads, formerly a near-monopoly for newspapers, and the loyalty of the younger generation to bite-sized news accounts on hand-held devices. Newspapers were far from perfect in covering baseball, to be sure. Its major-league-sanctioned writers fraternity, the Baseball Writers Association of America, was entitled, elitist, and exclusionary, and still has a chokehold on the Hall of Fame voting. As one century turned into another, baseball writers increasingly hung together in big packs at one end of big-league clubhouses and formed cooperatives to transcribe managers' pre- and

Newspapers may be diminished in circulation and staff, but their sports sections can still give the reader the top stories of the day boldly and loudly.

postgame conferences and other interviews. Whatever happened to friendly competition? The very nature of the beat writer's job, once the most prized on most newspapers, devolved into a quick road to burnout with the daily demands for content, and a brutal travel schedule with the scribes no longer welcome on the teams' charter flights.

One by one, the print chronicling of the nation's oldest team sport has been cut back as newspapers folded, pulled out of following their local teams altogether in favor of cheaper, "hyper-local" sports coverage, or yanked their writers off the road to save at least $50,000 in annual travel costs. Far fewer papers from big-league markets opted to cover the World Series, a trend noted sadly by commissioner Bud Selig in 2009, just after the trough of the Great Recession. *The Wall Street Journal* reported on increasingly lonely pressboxes in '09, noting the Pittsburgh chapter of the Baseball Writers Association of America had shrunk to nine members from 20 in 1988.

The lost print coverage has not been replaced adequately. Neither have the lost jobs. There are newfangled online media companies and fan bloggers. But the latter, proliferating all over the web, are denied access by some teams simply because of the threat of rabble-rousing, questions about the bloggers' professionalism, or because they are not part of legacy, old-school media outlets.

The steady withdrawal of print outlets from the pressboxes actually was the second wave of baseball coverage cutbacks in the past two decades. Most major AM and FM radio stations used to staff news departments with a sports mic jockey assigned to get tape at local events. But after deregulation of the radio industry in the 1990s, the stations no longer had to maintain the loss-leader news staff for public-service purposes.

On Baseball Scoops

"In the age of Twitter, almost nobody gets scoops anymore. Kenny Rosenthal [Fox] gets all the scoops. They get it from the agents." —*Bill Madden, former longtime* New York Daily News *baseball columnist and 2010 Spink Award winner at the Hall of Fame*

SPITBALLING

Even setting up a sports operation online in recent years is no guarantee of success. AOL did a relatively quick hook during the 2010s on several of its start-up media companies, including the sports site FanHouse. Fox Sports has had several big cutbacks in its existence.

Three J. G. Taylor Spink Award winners lost gigs in 2015, including Tom Gage, that year's award winner. Other victims were Cincinnati's Hal McCoy and New York's Bill Madden. Inclusion in the Hall of Fame writers' wing is not even assurance of job security anymore.

Overall, there is less competition for stories and less access to ballplayers and managers, and more choreographing of media availability by teams. Old-school managers didn't like the latter management tactic. Hall of Famer Bobby Cox and Jack McKeon preferred the jawboning of dugout banter to the stage-managed pre- and post-game press conferences. Despite the hand-wringing about coverage cuts by Selig, who used to hang out in Milwaukee County Stadium's pressbox to kibitz with writers, baseball is laughing its way to the bank in its protective, TV rights–fueled bubble. MLB Advanced Media, created after the sport centralized all team websites under one corporate roof in 2000, is one of the game's profit centers. Drawing more than 4 million hits today to a one-stop shop arrangement of game and feature stories, play-by-play of every pitch of every game in real time, live streaming of games and ticket outlets, MLBAM was called by Forbes.com in 2014 "The Biggest Media Company You've Never Heard Of." Revenues were $620 million a year in 2012 and climbing.

But for all its profitability and bells and whistles, BAM still cannot be as objective and independent as the old-fashioned newspaper baseball expert. Over the years, MLB.com writers admitted they had to adhere to some self-censorship on controversial stories.

The millennials lost something when they became absorbed in their hand-helds. The variety of coverage does not exist anymore.

As an example, in the late 1980s and early 1990s, the Dodgers' traveling press contingent was just about baseball's biggest. Characters like Gordon Verrell, Ken Gurnick, and Terry Johnson prowled clubhouses nationwide as the *Los Angeles Times*, *Los Angeles Herald-Examiner*, *Los Angeles Daily News*, *Orange County Register*, *Long Beach Press-Telegram*, *Torrance Daily Breeze*, *Riverside Press Enterprise*, and *San Bernardino Sun* offered varying degrees of road coverage. But by 2009, only the *Times* took to the road, and the Dodgers, in contrast to other big-market teams, began credentialing fan bloggers both as a nod to the changing times and to ensure multiple outlets continued writing about the team.

The brave new world of baseball media offers lots of sizzle, but far less steak than the good ol' days.

The brave new world of baseball media offers lots of sizzle, but far less steak than the good ol' days.

Batting Helmets

Evolution of Pumpkin Protectors Leads Back to the Pitcher's Mound

The 2014 season marked the first in which a pitcher—New York Mets lefty reliever Alex Torres—employed a Major League Baseball–approved padded hat as protection against liners back to the mound. That unusual-looking headgear, which caused the Twitter universe to light up, follows a game-wide effort to protect coaches from liners by mandating helmets while they work the baselines.

A new and apparently improved version was worn at the start of the 2015 campaign by Torres with the padding on the outside, courtesy of 4Licensing Corp., whose subsidiary Pinwrest makes the padding. The latest model, approved by MLB and the Players Association, shifted the padding from a bulkier placement on the inside to the outside of the cap.

"I liked more the one I used last year," said Torres. "I think if I use it [the new model] more and more games, I think I'm going to get a better feeling."

Whether pitchers will continue to tempt fate and trust their reactions over the 60-feet, 6-inch distance or cut down the risk will be the continuing story of protective headgear.

Given the care that the game takes for safeguarding pitchers and coaches to supplement the standard batting helmet, the standards for protection make the many decades through the 1950s where no on-field participant sported protective gear seem ignorant, if not outright careless, by comparison.

The evolution of batting helmets has progressed to where some players, such as the Cardinals' Jason Heyward, employ faceguards to protect formerly injured areas.

Players literally risked their lives in an era of comparative witch-doctor medicine by standing in without batting helmets. Errant pitches inevitably would strike a few hitters in the head or face. A couple of legends from the 1880s suggested some batters struck in the head came back with some form of a helmet, and were met with derision from their macho colleagues.

The first documented experiment with a helmet called a Head Protector was employed in 1907 by New York Giants catcher Roger Bresnahan after he was beaned. Bresnahan was forward-thinking about protection in every way. On Opening Day 1907, he became the first catcher to wear a mask, chest protector, and shin guards in a regular season game.

Other flirtations with head protection, including one by Cubs legend Frank Chance, were recorded over the next decade. Then the death of the Indians' Ray Chapman in 1920 after being hit by a Carl Mays pitch focused attention again on workable batting helmets.

But in almost every attempt to develop the headgear, players resisted based on comfort or vision issues, or adherence to an ancient manly baseball code.

How hockey goalies went without masks until the 1960s is a miracle; at least umpires and catchers long had common sense to protect themselves.

Resistance was firm, even after Hall of Fame catcher Mickey Cochrane and Joe Medwick suffered serious beanings in the years leading up to World War II. Experiments with cap liners did not gain wide acceptance.

Noted innovator Branch Rickey mandated his Pittsburgh Pirates wear plastic helmets in 1953, but both the Buccos and fans derided the adornments. The players were compared to coal miners and polo players.

By now, however, momentum was squarely in favor of helmets. In 1958, both leagues required helmets or liners inside their caps. Within a decade, the liners totally gave way to acceptance of hard-shell helmets, which officially became mandatory for hitters in 1971.

Still, complete protection was not possible. Hazards and catastrophic injuries abounded for both pitchers and batters at each end of the pitched/batted baseball. Top Cleveland lefty Herb Score was never really the same after being struck in the face by a liner off the bat of the Yankees' Gil McDougald in 1957. In 1967, Tony Conigliaro's superstar-trending career for the Red Sox was sidetracked when the Angels' Jack Hamilton hit him in the face with a pitch.

Increasingly, players adopted an ear flap, extending the protection of the helmet to the side of the head facing the pitcher to protect their faces. Then, as the millennium turned, the logical extension of the ear flap was developed with facemasks for wary players who had been hit in unprotected parts of their head. How hockey goalies went without masks until the 1960s is a miracle; at least umpires and catchers long had common sense to protect themselves. Now injured batters would add protection.

Interesting, the goalie mask was the inspiration for a close cousin worn first by Blue Jays catcher Charlie O'Brien as the 20th century ended. Catchers formerly had worn their caps backward with masks attached, affording questionable protection for the head. When helmets became mandatory, the catchers wore them backwards with their masks attached to the front, leaving the sides of the head still exposed to foul tips, wild pitches, or hitters' backswings. But the O'Brien mask-helmet, made of high-tech polycarbon, protected the top, sides, and back of the catcher's head. Meanwhile, the mask was designed to deflect the ball rather than accepting a direct hit like traditional masks.

Somehow, baseball dodged another Chapman-like bullet until July 22, 2007. Former cup-of-coffee big leaguer Mike Coolbaugh had been working for three weeks as first base coach of the Tulsa Drillers, the Double-A affiliate of the Colorado Rockies. In the ninth inning of the July 22 game against the Arkansas Travelers, Coolbaugh was killed by a line drive off the bat of Drillers catcher Tino Sanchez. The liner struck him in the neck. Coolbaugh was pronounced dead soon afterward at the hospital. Cause of death was the destruction of Coolbaugh's vertebral artery, severing his brain from his spinal cord.

Before the lords of baseball officially acted, some big-league first base and third base coaches immediately took action, wearing batting helmets for the rest of the 2007 season. The coaches' use of helmets became mandatory in following seasons.

But the need for protection for pitchers remained. Several big names such as the Dodgers' Clayton Kershaw were felled by liners back to the mound. Compounding the problem was the follow-through of many hurlers that rendered them virtually defenseless against the blue darts coming back at them. The end result was the padded caps as modeled by Torres.

Pitchers still aren't likely to wear helmets or affix facemasks to their caps. But it's a case of better late than never. The one part of baseball that is potentially deadly has been mitigated by the advance of technology and the dampening down of silly macho attitudes from a bygone age.

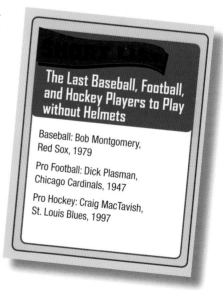

The Last Baseball, Football, and Hockey Players to Play without Helmets

Baseball: Bob Montgomery, Red Sox, 1979

Pro Football: Dick Plasman, Chicago Cardinals, 1947

Pro Hockey: Craig MacTavish, St. Louis Blues, 1997

Arthroscopy
No More Hobbled Patients

You can safely call Andre Dawson the poster child for arthroscopic surgery.

The Hall of Fame outfielder enjoyed a 20-year career from 1976 to 1996. But Dawson likely would not have gone that distance had the minimally invasive procedure commonly adopted for the meat of his career in the 80s not been available.

"I was cut [major surgery] twice, and had ten 'scopes,'" Dawson said of his ravaged knees that were somehow patched up efficiently to send him back out on the field through his career journeys to Montreal, Chicago, Boston, and Miami.

NO. 50

Initially, Dawson had major surgery to repair the medial ligament and meniscus on his left knee after playing high school football in his native Miami. He then had several arthroscopic procedures before undergoing another major surgery, when a bone spur was causing his right knee to lock.

"I did 'scopes later on because of the wear and tear on the cartilage and playing bone on bone," he said. "It caused degenerative changes in arthritis and bone spurs. I favored the knee on the AstroTurf, and I wore down the right knee, and that eventually caused me to have arthroscopy on that knee as well."

No way could Dawson have withstood more major knee surgeries and emerged mobile at all on the diamond. And that was the effect of the advent of arthroscopy, not as glamorous or singularly career-saving as Tommy John surgery, which involved the transplant of body parts. Arthroscopy did not make players run faster (Tommy John reportedly allowed pitchers with a new no-mileage elbow to throw a bit harder). But it did permit quicker recoveries and cut down on the loss of range of motion. Most importantly, the operation eliminated the trauma of cutting through healthy tissue to get to the afflicted area, ending the process of hobbling the patient in order to save him.

Andre Dawson (right), who had 10 arthroscopic knee surgeries, greets longtime Wrigley Field clubhouse boss Yosh Kawano in 2004.

"The advent of arthroscopy or minimally invasive surgery in baseball players clearly has revolutionized medicine and the game itself," said Dr. Charles Bush-Joseph, professor of orthopedic surgery and associate director of the Rush Orthopedic Sports Medicine Fellowship in Chicago.

"When pitchers had [major] shoulder injury, the procedure was to cut the muscles to get inside the joint. Those players were never the same. The trauma or morbidity of the surgery itself often times exceeded the benefit of what the surgery was doing. If a pitcher had an unstable shoulder or labral tear, if you cut the muscle tissues to get into the shoulder, just the nature of cutting the muscle, the players would lose 15 degrees on average of getting their arm up and throwing in that 90-90 position. Now the likelihood of losing motion after surgery has gone down dramatically."

Every player needs his legs to survive. Tearing of anterior cruciate ligaments (ACLs) in knees used to be a catastrophic injury. Now through 'scopes, the original damage is more efficiently repaired while the recovery time has been cut.

You see players getting back five, six, seven months after surgery as opposed to 12 to 15 months in the old days.

Bush-Joseph can directly relate to every ACL patient with whom he has dealt. Both of his ACLs have been reconstructed.

"The ability to do it arthroscopically dramatically lessens the morbidity of the surgery," Bush-Joseph said. "The patient is not immobilized, we can move the joint, we are not cutting into the muscle. Instead of having severe atrophy after surgery due to immobilization, we can mobilize the patient right away and lower that atrophy. That's why you see players getting back five, six, seven months after surgery as opposed to 12 to 15 months in the old days. Then, players would be in a cast six weeks after surgery and would take them two years to get their muscle mass back."

The surgeries Dawson underwent and young physician Bush-Joseph performed in the late 1980s have dramatically advanced into a new century. "I don't do a single operation like I did in 1988," Bush-Joseph said of the year he finished his surgical training. "The techniques and equipment and rehab have advanced so far in 28 years. That's where physicians have to be responsible for their continuing education. A physician needs 120 hours every other year just to maintain his professional certification. I teach residents and fellows and practicing surgeons how to advance techniques, and allow our athletes to have re-producible outcomes."

What does not change is the human spirit. The hardest workers who toil through grueling rehab sessions are most often rewarded.

"Three or four times I had the 'scope during the season," Dawson said. "Several times in

On Playing through Discomfort

"I played under discomfort the entirety of my career. There was some degree of pain associated with discomfort, but I was able to block that out. And I got better and better with that as the years passed to where I could go out and play with that discomfort." —*Hall of Famer Andre Dawson*

SPITBALLING

Montreal, once in Chicago, once in Boston. Recovery was four to six weeks. Shortest one was in Boston. The Red Sox went on a 13-day road trip. I had surgery the first day of the trip [in Boston]. I knew the procedure as far as physical therapy. I went to Fenway every day. I did the routine, stretching, ice, bending the knee. I did not do running. When they returned from the road trip, I was ready to go out and play. They couldn't believe what they were seeing. They didn't want to have me go back on field, but I persuaded them. I went through agility tests—running bases, sprints, starts and stopping. We did that over a two-day period and they were convinced I could go out and play. But they would only let me DH."

Dawson had learned the hard way the necessity of strenuous rehab and physical therapy. He unfortunately set up his series of operations after his first major surgery in high school.

"I did not do physical therapy as a 17-year-old," he said. "I never really regained my range of motion on my left knee. After surgery, it was 'I'll see you in two weeks' from the doctor. I had a cast on, and a lot of atrophy when the cast was removed. Not doing rehab, I put a knee brace on and kind of limped around until I regained the strength. Had I initially done the physical therapy, that could have eliminated a lot of problems with the other knee and the damaged knee as well."

Bush-Joseph said the next frontier of injury recovery will not be with surgical instruments. "We're entering the age of biologics in medicine," he said. "We enhance the healing and reproduce better healing tissue whether it's manipulating the healing process or adding elements or stem cells to the healing process that we didn't do before. Virtually 95 percent of orthopedic investigation in sports medicine now deals more with the biological aspects of healing as opposed to the mechanical nature of the techniques."

ACKNOWLEDGMENTS OF A TRUE TEAM EFFORT

I'd call myself a tape archaeologist, pulling in from left field long-lost audio- and videotape of baseball game action and interviews that you'd think was never saved, but in fact was recorded by some far-flung fan.

But while building *Baseball's Game Changers* chapter-by-chapter, photo-by-photo, I never figured the Harrison Ford in me would extend to the still lifes of the game.

As I extend thanks to a veritable 40-person roster who assisted with this book, a primary appreciation must go out to three people who helped bring a spectacular historical photo to these pages.

For decades, I was aware of a photo taken by Earl Gustie in the *Chicago Tribune*'s color studio in Tribune Tower early in 1960. The image portrays the Cubs' Ernie Banks and the White Sox's Nellie Fox, fresh from receiving their respective leagues' 1959 Most Valuable Player Awards, posing around a giant TK-41 color TV camera with WGN baseball announcer Jack Brickhouse. The photo, originally shot for the April 9, 1960 *Tribune*'s TV Week Saturday weekly supplement, promoted the inauguration of WGN's color telecasts of Cubs and White Sox games. WGN was the second local station in the country to air baseball in tint after Cincinnati's WLWT for Reds games in 1959, and five years after NBC began color broadcasts of World Series games.

The Banks-Fox-Brickhouse photo was published in the *Tribune* on several occasions in the not-distant past. Individuals also possessed copies. But when I requested the use of the photo from the newspaper itself, top editors Mark Jacob and Robin Daughtridge could not locate a copy in the files despite an exhaustive search.

Good fortune is always welcome, though. Somehow, I stumbled upon the photo in the holdings of Danon Gallery, an art house with a modest sports photo collection, in Evanston, Illinois. As an intermediary between owner Bob Danon—still proud of his youthful days as a Chicago ballpark vendor in 1962—and Jacob and Daughtridge, I arranged a return of the photo to its original owner. The end result of that process is being able to share that photo with you as part of our Television chapter.

Jacob, Daughtridge, and Danon weren't the only folks expending energy on our behalf. Comcast SportsNet Chicago's Jeff Nuich, one of the best media relations persons in the country, and CSN Chicago production chief Jim Corno Jr. arranged a photo shoot of their baseball production crew for several video-oriented chapters here. CSN Chicago boss Phil Bedella and top producers Sarah Lauch and Ryan McGuffey are also quoted in these pages.

A gaggle of big-league team media relations officials, archivists, and photographers came through big-time responding to requests. Included were the Angels' Tim Mead and Matt Birch; the Twins' Dustin Morse and Brace Hemmelgarn; the Marlins' P. J. Loyello and Robert Vigon; the Red Sox's Kevin Gregg and Michael Ivins; the Yankees' Jason Zillo; the Pirates' Dan Hart; the Dodgers' Mark Langill, and the Athletics' Adam Loberstein. And, as usual, Chicago Baseball Museum webmaster Carol Kneedler was lightning fast in response to fulfilling photo requests.

A particular shout-out goes to Hall of Famers who were most patient with me. Leading the pack was true gentleman Andre Dawson, who returns calls in a manner not often seen in the 21st century. No wonder Dawson was the first enshrinee asked by the Hall of Fame to help escort President Barack Obama in his 2014 tour through Cooperstown's displays. Goose Gossage was opinionated as usual. Reds voice Marty Brennaman, a past Ford Frick Award winner in the Hall's announcers' wing, sported the same candid style off the air as on. A profound session was with fellow Frick honoree Milo Hamilton, who shared his thoughts four months prior to his September 2015 passing.

Speaking of the Hall of Fame, photo archivists John Horne and Ken Roussey were their usual helpful personas. John Thorne, Major League Baseball's official historian, led the way to some important sources of research. As usual, the Morton Grove and Skokie (IL) public libraries lent their assistance.

Meanwhile, Charlotte's Leigh-Ann Young, amid her own quest to find a tape of her late father Rube Walker's voice, was most gracious in tapping into the elder Walker's historic photo collection. Much closer to home, wife Nina Castle and daughter Laura Castle were Tony Phillips–type utility players, doing a little bit of this, a little bit of that in assisting an often-tech-challenged author. This time, Laura added her first-ever photo credit. My books, dating back to 1998, have truly been family projects.

In the long, sometimes lonely hours of transcribing and writing, man's best friend is invaluable as companion and informal doorkeeper. I'll pay tribute here to a beautiful, petite basset hound named Abby, long my "chief office dog," who passed away much too young of a sudden illness while I wrote this book. Laura's dog Kona and a new family addition, Patches, a strikingly handsome border collie mix, are in training for the "office dog" job.

Last, but never least, is my double-play partner, Lyons Press editor Keith Wallman, collaborating for his third book with me. Keith and I know each other's moves almost by heart. Every author should have an editor as conscientious as Keith.

INDEX

PHOTO CREDITS

"Spitballing" sidebar illustration by Aaron H. Dana

--

Panel page, Bob Gibson: National Baseball Hall of Fame Library, Roe, Cooperstown, N.Y.; p. x: Courtesy of Chris Krug; p. xi: cosmin4000/iStock/Thinkstock

Scukrov/iStock/Thinkstock, p. v

--

No. 5, 1919 White Sox: Courtesy of the Chicago Baseball Museum; background: Library of Congress; p. 4, Buck Weaver: Courtesy of the Chicago Baseball Museum

No. 4, Marvin Miller: National Baseball Hall of Fame Library, Cooperstown, N.Y.; background: Comstock/Stockbyte/Thinkstock

No. 3, Banks, Fox, and Brickhouse: Earl Gustie photograph courtesy of the *Chicago Tribune*; background: BradCalkins/iStock/Thinkstock

No. 2, Jackie Robinson comic book: Library of Congress

No. 1, Babe Ruth: Library of Congress; background: Library of Congress

--

No. 6, AL club presidents 1914: Library of Congress

No. 7, 1895 "base ball" poster: Library of Congress

No. 8, Rickey, Hornsby, and Breadon: National Baseball Hall of Fame Library, Cooperstown, N.Y.; background: Alexandru Dobrea/Hemera/Thinkstock

No. 9, Minnie Minoso: National Baseball Hall of Fame Library, LOOK (Lerner), Cooperstown, N.Y.; p. 44, Jose Abreu: Photo by George Castle

No. 10, Charlie Sprague card: Library of Congress; background: Jupiterimages/liquidlibrary/Thinkstock

No. 11, Bill Mazeroski: Courtesy of the Pittsburgh Pirates; background: Hemera Technologies/AbleStock.com/Thinkstock

No. 12, Andy Messersmith: National Baseball Hall of Fame Library, Cooperstown, N.Y.; p. 56, Walter O'Malley: Courtesy of the Los Angeles Dodgers

No. 13, Tony La Russa and Mike Rizzo: Photo by George Castle; p. 60, Goose Gossage and Pete War: Photo by George Castle

No. 14, Bob Gibson: National Baseball Hall of Fame Library, Roe, Cooperstown, N.Y.

No. 15, Tony Oliva batting: Courtesy of the Minnesota Twins Baseball Club; p. 68, Tony Oliva fielding: Courtesy of the Minnesota Twins Baseball Club

No. 16, Crosley Field: National Baseball Hall of Fame Library, Payne, Cooperstown, N.Y

No. 17, Red Sox celebration: © Julie Cordeiro / Boston Red Sox

No. 18, Marlins celebration: © Marlins, Denis Bancroft; background: Randy Hines/iStock/ Thinkstock

No. 19, Tommy John and Dr. Frank Jobe: Courtesy of the Los Angeles Dodgers; background: tomasworks/iStock/Thinkstock

No. 20, Bert Blyleven: Courtesy of the Minnesota Twins Baseball Club

No. 21, replay equipment: Courtesy of Comcast SportsNet Chicago

No. 22, Marty Brennaman: Photo by George Castle

No. 23, Dodgers and White Sox: Courtesy of the Los Angeles Dodgers; background: AugiCA/ iStock/Thinkstock

No. 24, Gene Autry: Courtesy of Angels Baseball

No. 25, Astrodome: Library of Congress

No. 26, Willie Wilson: National Baseball Hall of Fame Library, Sauritch, Cooperstown, N.Y.

No. 27, Maury Wills: Courtesy of the Los Angeles Dodgers; background: joephotographer/ iStock/Thinkstock

No. 28, Johnny Bench: National Baseball Hall of Fame Library, Raphael, Cooperstown, N.Y.

No. 29, Angels celebration: Courtesy of Angels Baseball; background: Library of Congress

p. 124, Angels celebration: Courtesy of Angels Baseball

No. 30, Curt Flood: National Baseball Hall of Fame Library, Cooperstown, N.Y.

No. 31, Bruce Sutter: National Baseball Hall of Fame Library, Cooperstown, N.Y.

No. 32, Mark McGwire and Sammy Sosa: National Baseball Hall of Fame Library, Vesely, Cooperstown, N.Y.

No. 33, Randy Johnson: National Baseball Hall of Fame Library, Mangin, Cooperstown, N.Y.

No. 34, Frank Robinson and Verlon "Rube" Walker: Courtesy of Leigh-Ann Young

No. 35, Reggie Jackson and Hank Aaron: Library of Congress

No. 36, Michael Jordan: © Bill Smith Photography

No. 37, Barry Bonds: Courtesy of the Pittsburgh Pirates

No. 38, Billy Beane: Courtesy of the Oakland A's/Travis LoDolce

No. 39, George Steinbrenner: Photo by William Coupon/New York Yankees — © New York Yankees. All Rights Reserved.

No. 40, Fenway Park: Photo by Laura Castle; p. 168, Genevieve Ebbets: Library of Congress

No. 41, Camden Yards: Library of Congress

No. 42, William L. Veeck and Margaret Donahue: Courtesy of the Chicago Baseball Museum; background: chepatchet/iStock/Thinkstock

No. 43, Bill Veeck: Author's Collection

No. 44, Carlton Fisk: Photo by Dennis Brearley/ © Boston Red Sox; background: Library of Congress

No. 45, Dodgers and Angels fans: Courtesy of Angels Baseball; p. 188, Dodgers and Angels players: Courtesy of Angels Baseball

No. 46, television remote truck: Courtesy of Comcast SportsNet Chicago; p. 193, baseball TV director: Courtesy of Comcast SportsNet Chicago

No. 47, center field camera shot: Courtesy of Comcast SportsNet Chicago; background: Courtesy of Comcast SportsNet Chicago; p. 196, Little League TV ad: Author's Collection

No. 48, newspapers: Mitrija/iStock/Thinkstock

No. 49, Jason Heyward: National Baseball Hall of Fame Library, Fruth, Cooperstown, N.Y.

No. 50, Andre Dawson and Yosh Kawano: Photo by George Castle; background: Library of Congress

ABOUT THE AUTHOR

George Castle witnessed and/or covered many of the "Game Changers" chronicled in this book over a lifetime watching baseball in his native Chicago and on road trips coast to coast.

Growing up in the cheap seats at Wrigley Field and old Comiskey Park, Castle eventually switched to the pressbox for a 35-year career chronicling baseball, along with offseason diversions such as the NHL and NBA. He's worked for newspapers, magazines, and online sites. From 1994 to 2010, he hosted and produced *Diamond Gems*, a weekly syndicated baseball radio program. And he has served as historian for the Chicago Baseball Museum.

Baseball's Game Changers is his 13th book overall since 1998 and fourth for Lyons Press. He also has written four children's books focused on teams' histories.

He lives in Chicago's northern suburbs with wife Nina, border collie mix Patches, and 23-year-old African Grey parrot Casey. Daughter Laura, a contributor to this book, acquired her love of baseball from the old man.

One "game changer" he has not witnessed much in Chicago are multiple World Series championships.

ALSO BY GEORGE CASTLE

When the Game Changed: An Oral History of Baseball's True Golden Age: 1969–1979
Throwbacks: Old-School Baseball Players in Today's Game
Baseball and the Media: How Fans Lose in Today's Coverage of the Game
The Million-to-One Team: Why the Chicago Cubs Haven't Won a Pennant Since 1945
The I-55 Series: Cubs vs. Cardinals
Entangled in Ivy: Inside the Cubs' Quest for October
Sweet Lou and the Cubs: A Year Inside the Dugout
Where Have All Our Cubs Gone?